BUDGETING AND BUDGETARY CONTROL

Toye Adelaja

INTRODUCTION

Budgeting is the financial planning and preparation for the potential activity of a business. The planning can be a short-term planning, a medium-term planning or a long-term planning.

A short-term financial planning which can also be referred to as short-term budget may not require large amount of fund, but a long-term financial planning or long-term budgeting requires a large amount of finance.

Short-term Budgeting is a financial or quantitative plan of operation of an organization for a **forthcoming accounting period**.

Long-term budgeting or capital expenditure budgeting involves decisions regarding acquisition of fixed assets, and other long-term projects of a company. Such decisions include acquisition of equipment and machinery, acquisition of land and buildings, introduction of new products and so on.

Table of Contents

Chapters		Pages
1	Budget	4
2	Types and Preparation of Budgets	10
3	Budgets Preparation and Approval Techniques	21
4	Techniques used in Budgeting	43
5	Forecasting and Budgetary Control	56
6	Capital Expenditure Planning and Control	61
7	Investments Appraisal Techniques	66
8	Non-discount Cash Flow Techniques	68
9	Concepts in Capital Budgeting Decisions	75
10	Discounted Cash Flow Techniques	80
11	Complex Investment Decisions	99
12	Capital Rationing	110

CHAPTER 1

1.0 BUDGET

Learning Objectives

In this chapter, readers should be able to:

(i) understand the meaning of budgets

(ii) distinguish between budget and capital budgeting

(iii) understand various terms of budgets

(iv) know purposes of budgets

1.1 What is a budget?

A budget can be prepared for a person, a family, a business, government and a non-profit oriented organization. For the purpose of this study, we shall be discussing on a business budget. A Budget can be simply defined in the following ways:

A Budget is a financial or quantitative plan of operation of an organization for a **forthcoming accounting period**.

It is defined as a quantitative and/or a financial statement for a **definite future period**; which may include planned income, expenditures, assets, liabilities and cash flows. It provides a focus and direction for an organization. It aids the coordination of activities and facilitates evaluation of performances in an organization.

It is a financial and/or quantitative statement of planned income and expenditure.

It is a financial and/or quantitative statement of planned assets and liabilities.

It is a financial statement of planned cash flow or cash flow projection.

It is common that the budgets prepared for the next accounting year will be detailed by quarter and/or month.

It is an estimate of revenues and expenditures for specified future period of time.

Budgeting is the process of creating a budget.

A budget which is commonly known as a short-term financial planning (budget) is different from a capital budgeting which may be known as a medium-term financial planning or a long-term financial planning. Capital budgeting can be explained in the context of a firm's decision to invest its current funds in long term activities in anticipation of an expected flow of future benefits over a number of years. However, the investment decisions could be in the form of acquisition of additional fixed assets, replacements and modifications of activities or expansion of a plant.

1.2 Purposes of a budget

Purposes of a business budget are as follows:

COMMUNICATION

It serves as a means of communicating ideas, plans and goals to the people concerned. It enables each member of staff to know what to do. Communication might be one-way, that is, with managers giving order to subordinates, or there might be a two-way dialogue and exchange of ideas, this is between managers and subordinates.

CO-ORDINATION
It coordinates the activities of different departments or sub-units of the organization towards the achievement of the organizational set goals and objectives. For example, a purchasing department should base its budget on production requirements, and the production budget should be determined by the expected sales.

CONTROL
Budget establishes a system of control by having a planned result compared with the actual result and variance (difference) is determined for prompt action and attention.

PLANNING
Budget is prepared in order to plan for the future. Where a new business is to be commenced, there should be a proper planning of the business. The planning may include number of employees required, the location and size of the office building, number and cost of fixed assets such as computers, plant and machinery, fixtures and fittings etc. to be used. Budget can also be prepared by an existing business to plan for the future expenditure and income. The budget can be prepared using previous records of the business to predict financial operation for the future.

MOTIVATION

Budget is used to motivate each member of staff in each department to work towards the achievement of the departmental goals in particular and towards the organization goals in general

LOAN FACILITY
Budget can also be prepared to obtain loans from financial institution. If the budget prepared is reasonable to the lender of loans, the loans will be made available provided other requirements are met.

1.3 Functions of Budget

Budget are designed to carry out varieties of functions such as planning, co-ordinations of activities, implementing plans, communication, evaluating performances, motivation and authorization action.

1.4. Budget Period

Budgeting must be related to a specific period of time. Budget may be prepared for the next year. This may be subdivided into monthly periods for proper monitoring and control.

Many organizations review and modify their budgets on a continuous basis because of rapidly changing economical and technological conditions. Typically, budgets are reviewed each quarter or half year. Budgets can also be reviewed for the following twelve months.

1.5 Limiting Factor or Principal Budget Factor

There are some factors that must be considered before a budget is prepared. These factors are called limiting factors. They are the factors that will prevent a budget from being attained. These factors are as follows:

1. Demand by customers
2. Production capacity
3. Shortage of human power
4. Shortage of raw materials
5. Financial constraints
6. Space.

All these factors should be carefully identified and the effect on each budget carefully considered during budget preparation process.

1.6 Budget Manual

Budget Manual contains information and guidance about budgetary processes. It facilitates flow of communication about objectives of budgeting. It does not contain a budget for a particular period. It is more of instructional manual and information about how a budget operates in an organization.

The contents of budget manual vary from organization to organization. The following are common information it should contain:

1. Objectives and explanation of the budgeting processes
    I. explanation of the budgeting planning and control
    II. objective of each stage of budgetary process
    III. relationship to long term planning

2. Organization structure and responsibilities
    I. titles and names of current budget holders
    II. Structure of the organization showing titles, responsibility and relationship

3. Main budgets and their relationship

I. outlines of all main budgets and their accounting relationship
   II. explanation of key budgets (e. g Master budget, cash budget, sales budget)

5. Budget development
   I. budget committee, membership and terms of references
   II. sequence of budget preparation
   III. time table for budget preparation and publication

6. Accounting procedures
   I. Names of budget officer (usually the accountant)

CHAPTER 2

TYPES AND PREPARATION OF BUDGET

Learning objectives

In this chapter, the readers should be able to:

(i) understand functional budgets

(ii) know differences between functional budgets and master budgets

(iii) know how to prepare various functional budgets

2.0 Classification of Budgets

Budget can be classified into two main groups. They are functional budgets and master budget.

2.1. Functional Budgets

Functional budget is prepared by each departmental head. The nature of an organization determines the types of departments in the organization. A manufacturing company may have production department, purchasing department, sales department, marketing department and accounting department. Each of the departments in an organization must present a departmental budget called functional budget.

The order of importance in the preparation of budget is determined by budget limiting factors of the organization. Where sales are considered critical to the success of the objective of the organization, sales budget should be prepared first. Similarly, where there is a limited supply of raw materials, raw material budget should be prepared first.

2.2 Types of Functional Budget

In every business entity, there must be two or more departments. Budget should be prepared for each of the departments. Budget prepared for each of the departments is called functional budget. For example, the various functional budges that should be prepared in a typical manufacturing company are as follows:

	Functional Budgets	Meaning
1	Sales Budget	Expected Sales
2	Production Budget	Expected Production requirement
3	Direct Material Purchase budget	Expected raw material needed
4	Direct labor cost	Amount of money expected to be spent on direct labor
5	Overhead Budget	Amount of money planned to be spent on indirect expenses
6	Marketing Budget	Amount of money planned to be spent on marketing.

The co-ordination and compilation of all the functional budgets into a single budget is called **Master Budget.** The following are the types of Functional Budgets:

2.2.1 Direct Raw Material Purchase Budget

Direct raw material purchase budget is an estimate of raw material needed to achieve a desired level of production; the production budget.

In raw materials purchase budget, quantity of each of the materials to buy is calculated. The following determine quantity to buy:

a. Number of each of the units needed for production.
b. Number of units expected to remain at the end of the period (closing inventory of raw materials)
c. Number of units of each of the materials already in stock (opening inventory of raw materials)

The quantity of raw material purchase budget is calculated as follows:

Quantity of raw material required for production + Closing inventory of raw material desired – opening inventory of raw material

The formula above can also be used to determine quantity of finished goods purchase budget, but every raw material in the formula will be changed to finished goods.

ILLUSTRATION

Samotex Plc. is a multi-product company producing APP, TMA and EMA from two different materials (cotton-wool and dye).

Each unit of APP requires 2 units of cotton wool and 2 units of dye. Each unit of TMA requires 3 units of cotton wool and 4 units of dye. Each unit of EMA requires 1 unit of cotton wool and 5 units of dye. Production during the year 1998 is expected to be 10,000 units of APP, 2,500 units of TMA and 3,000 units of EMA. Inventory of raw materials as at 31/12/97 are:

Cotton wool   500 units

Dye   1,000 units

It is the company's policy to make closing inventory of each type of material 10% higher than opening inventory. Purchase price per unit are cotton wool $14 and Dye $25.

You are required to:

a) Prepare the company's raw material purchase budget for 1998
b) Prepare the company's raw material cost budget for 1998

SOLUTION
a)
Raw material purchase (quantity) budget for 1998

	cotton wool	Dye
	Units	Units
Quantity needed for production	30,500	45,000
Add: Closing inventory desired	550	1,100
	31,050	46,100
Less: Opening inventory	(500)	(1,000)
Quantity to buy	30,550	45,100

b)
Raw material cost budget for 1998

	cotton wool	Dye
	Units	Units
Quantity needed for production	30,500	45,000
Add: Closing inventory desired	550	1,100
	31,050	46,100
Less: Opening inventory	(500)	(1,000)
Quantity to buy	30,550	45,100
Cost per unit	$14	$25
	30,550 × $14	45,100 × $25
	$	$
Raw material cost budget	427,700	$1,127,500

WORKINGS:

Raw material quantity required to be used for each product are as follows:

APP

Cotton wool; 2units×1×10,000 units = 20,000 units

Dye;   2units ×1×10,000 units = 20,000 units

Note:

    a) 1 unit of APP requires 2 units of cotton wool (2units of cotton wool × 1unit of App).

b) 10,000 units of APP are needed to be produced. The number of cotton wool that will be used for the production will be; 2units of cotton wool × 1 unit of APP × 10,000 units of APP = 20,000 units of cotton wool

c) 1unit of APP requires 2 units of dye (2units of dye × 1unit of App).

d) 10,000 units of APP are needed to be produced. The number of dye that will be used for the production will be; 2units of dye × 1 unit of APP × 10,000 units of APP = 20,000 units of dye

TMA

Cotton wool; 3×1× 2,500 units = 7,500 units
Dye;   4 ×1× 2500 units = 10,000 units

Note:

a) 1unit of TMA requires 3 units of cotton wool (3units of cotton wool × 1unit of TMA).

b) 2,500 units of TMA are needed to be produced. The number of cotton wool that will be used for the production will be; 3units of cotton wool × 1 unit of TMA × 2,500 units of TMA = 7,500 units of cotton wool

c) 1unit of TMA requires 4 units of dye (4units of dye × 1unit of TMA).

d) 2,500 units of TMA are needed to be produced. The number of dye that will be used for the production will be; 4units of dye × 1 unit of TMA × 2,500 units of TMA = 10,000 units of dye

EMA

Cotton wool; 1×1× 3,000 units =3,000 units
Dye;   5×1× 3,000 units = 15,000 units

Raw materials needed for production

	APP units	TMA Units	EMA units	Total units
Cotton wool	20,000	7,500	3,000	30,500
Dye	20,000	10,000	15,000	45,000

NOTE:
The raw material budget above is meant for a financial year 1998 (period) as a whole. A budget can be prepared for each sub-period such as monthly, quarterly and semi-annually.

ILLUSTRATION 2

Sunday Ltd. uses two set of raw materials; material "A" and "B" in producing a product and has estimated the following quantity of raw materials to be used for the next four quarter:

	A Units	B Units
Quarter 1	24,000	26,000
Quarter 2	32,000	34,000
Quarter 3	26,000	28,000

| Quarter 4 | 20,000 | 20,000 |

The opening raw materials at the beginning of quarter "1" is 2,600 units for "A" and 3,000 units for "B". The management has decided that the closing inventory in a quarter should be 10% of the quantity of raw materials expected to be used in the next period. Prepare raw materials purchase budget for quarter 1, 2 and 3.

SOLUTION:

Sunday Ltd.

Raw material "A" purchase budget for the next 3 quarters

	Quarter 1 Units	Quarter 2 Units	Quarter 3 Units
Raw material required	24,000	32,000	26,000
Add: Closing inventory	3,200	2,600	2,000
	27,200	34,600	28,000
Less: Opening inventory	-2,600	-3,200	-2,600
Raw materials purchase	24,600	31,400	25,400

Raw material "B" purchase budget for the next 3 quarters

	Quarter 1 Units	Quarter 2 Units	Quarter 3 Units
Raw material required	26,000	34,000	28,000
Add: Closing inventory	3,400	2,800	2,000
	29,400	36,800	30,000
Less: Opening inventory	-3,000	-3,400	-2,800
Raw materials purchase	26,400	33,400	27,200

2.2.2 Production Budget:
this is an estimate of quantities and number of units to be made in each factory or manufacturing/production department in order to meet expected sales. Production budget also includes the estimate of various costs such as raw material cost, labor cost and other expenses related to the production.

ILLUSTRATION 1

Smith Ltd. makes and sell one product and have estimated the following sales volumes for the next four periods.

Period 1   52,000units
Period 2   68,000units
Period 3   56,000units
Period 4   44,000units

The opening stock at beginning of period 1 is 5,700units. The managements have decided that the closing stock in each period should be 10% of the sales volume expected in the next period.
Your are required to prepare quantity production budget for period 1, 2, and 3

Solution

Smith Ltd. Quantity production budget for the next three periods

	Period 1 Units	Period 2 Units	Period 3 Units
Sales	52,000	68,000	56,000
Add: Closing Stock	6,800	5,600	4,400
	58,800	73,600	60,400
Less: Opening Stock	-5,700	-6,800	-5,600

| Production required | 53,100 | 66,800 | 54,800 |

The quantity production budget for the period 1, 2, 3 are as follows:

Period 1	53,100 units
Period 2	66,800 units
Period 3	54,800 units

2.2.3 Sales Budget: This involves the expected or estimated sales volume and unit prices for each item of product (or service) for all segments of the company's product or service.

ILLUSTRATION

VIGI PLC is a multi product company producing and selling three products TRA TMA and TIM. Sales for last quarter of 1997 had been:

TRA 30,000 units at $20
TMA 25,000 units at $28
TIM 60,000 units at $16

Past experience shows that sales quantity is increasing annually at a constant rate of 7%. Due to economic measure recently introduced by the government, prices are expected to rise in 1998 by 2%.

Required:

Prepare the company's sales budget for 1st Quarter of 1998

SOLUTION

TRA 107% of 30,000 = 32,100 units
TMA 107% of 25,000 = 26,750 units
TIM 107% of 60,000 = 64,200 units

1998 first quarter selling price are:
TRA 102% of $20 = $20.4
TMA 102% of $28 = $28.56
TIM 102% of $16 = $16.32

VIGI PLC
Sales Budget for 1st Quarter of 1998

Products	Quantity(units)	Price($)	Amount ($)
TRA	32,100	20.4	654,840
TMA	26,750	28.56	763,980
TIM	64,200	16.32	1,047,744
			2,466,564

2.2.4 Marketing budget: This is an estimate of funds required for promotion, marketing, advertising and public relation in order to create awareness about company's products and services.

2.2.5 Project Budget: This is a kind of budget that shows the prediction of the costs associated with each project a company is about to execute. These costs include material costs, labor costs and other related expenses.

CHAPTER 3

BUDGET PREPARATION AND APPROVAL TECHNIQUES

Learning Objectives

In this chapter, readers should be able to understand:

(i) Master budget

(ii) Cash Budgeting

(iii) Simple cash flow management

(iv) Operational and financial budget

3.0 Budget Preparation and Approval Techniques

3.1 Master Budget

Master Budget is a set of operating and financial budgets for a particular accounting period, usually the next fiscal or calendar year. Master budget is prepared monthly, quarterly and annually.

The format of master budget is determined by the nature and size of a business entity. Operating budgets are used in daily operation of an organization and are the basis for the preparation of financial budget.

Operating budgets are the income statements elements such as revenue, purchases, production, direct labor wages, direct materials cost, cost of goods manufactured, overheads and cost of goods sold.

Financial budgets include budgeted income statement, budgeted statement of financial position, cash budget and capital expenditures budget. Financial budget can also be viewed as a budget for statement of financial position elements. It deals with expected assets, liabilities and stockholders' equity.

Budgeted income Statement is an estimate of an organization's profit for a given budget period. Most organizations prepare budgeted income statement using the accrual basis of accounting: revenues are recorded when earned and expenses are recorded when incurred.

Capital expenditure budget is an estimate of fixed assets or long-term assets to be purchased during the budget period. These fixed assets include the plant and machinery, equipment, property, intangible assets such as trademarks, copyrights and patents. This budget should be carefully prepared and implemented because it requires huge amount of capital.

Budgeted Balance Sheet is the last piece of budget process. It is an estimate of the ending balance for all balance sheet items.

3.2 Budget Preparation Procedures

The business of an enterprise must be conducted in an orderly and efficient manner in order to achieve the desired result. Budgeting is a very critical part of management activities.

In practice, top management may constitute a budget committee which may comprise:
1. The Managing director/Chief Executive officer as the chairman.

2. Chief Accountant or Director of finance as the budget officer. He co-ordinates the preparation and readiness of other budgets and prepare cash budget as well as master budget.

3. Head of each department or a line manager who prepares a functional budget for each department.

It is necessary that management must hold a pre-budgeting meeting where the guidelines for new budget period are drafted, discussed and approved. This means that the new budget must meet the new standards and criteria.

3.3 Approval of Master Budget

The budget committee will submit the master budget to the top management (the board of directors) for approval. If it is approved, the master budget will become a blueprint for all the activities of the budgeted period. If the master budget is disapproved, parts of the budget will have to be amended to comply with the top management requirements. There must be an assurance that the new budget that would be produced after the amendment is realistic.

3.4 Preparation of Master Budget

It has been explained earlier that a master budget consolidates the position of all the functional budgets in the form of a budgeted income statement, a budgeted statement of financial position and cash budget. Master budget can be prepared in the following ways:

1. Each of the functional budgets can be prepared separately subject to co-ordination of a budget officer and subsequently consolidated into a master budget (budgeted income statement, budgeted statement of financial position and cash budget) by the Budget officer who is the chief accountant or director of finance. Some methods of preparing functional budgets have been explained in the chapter "2" of this book. The preparation of cash budget is the sole responsibility of a budget officer.

ILLUSTRATION 1

Smith chocolate produces chocolate for resale at grocery stores. The company is currently in process of establishing a master budget on a quarterly basis for this coming fiscal year, which ends December 31. Prior year quarterly sales were as follows:

1st quarter	32,000 units
2nd quarter	38,400 units
3rd quarter	48,000 units
4th quarter	41,600 units

Unit sales are expected to increase by 25%, and each unit is expected to sell for $8. The management prefers to maintain closing finished goods inventory equal to 10% of next quarter's expected sales. Assume finished goods inventory at the end of the fourth quarter budget period is estimated to be 4,500 units.
You are required to:

a) Prepare sales budget for Smith chocolate.
b) Prepare production budget for Smith chocolate

SOLUTION

a)

Figure 3.41 Smith Chocolate Sales Budget
For the year ending December 31

	Q1	Q2	Q3	Q4	Year
Prior year sales in units	32,000	38,400	48,000	41,600	160,000
Budget increase of 25%	× 1.25	× 1.25	× 1.25	× 1.25	
Expected sales in units	40,000	48,000	60,000	52,000	200,000
Unit price	× $8	× $8	× $8	× $8	
Expected sales values	320,000	384,000	480,000	416,000	1,600,000

b)

Figure 3.42 Smith Chocolate Production Budget
For the year ending December 31

	Q1	Q2	Q3	Q4	Year
Sales in unit	40,000	48,000	60,000	52,000	200,000
Add: Desired closing finished goods inventory	4,800	6,000	5,200	4,500	4,500
Total finished goods inventory needed	44,800	54,000	65,200	56,500	204,500
Opening finished goods inventory	-4,000	-4,800	-6,000	-5,200	-4,000
Units to be produced	40,800	49,200	59,200	51,300	200,500

Illustration 2

Smith Chocolate, the company featured in the last illustration and in the next 3, is now preparing budget for direct materials purchases, direct labor and manufacturing overheads.

Direct materials purchase budget information:

Each unit of production requires 1.5 pounds of direct materials per unit, and the cost of direct materials is $2 per pound. Management prefers to maintain closing raw materials inventory equal to 30 per cent of next quarter's materials needed in production. Assume raw materials inventory at end of the fourth quarter budget period is estimated to be 20,500 pounds.

Direct labor Budget information:

Each unit of product requires 0.2 direct labor hour at a cost of $12 per hour.

Manufacturing overhead budget information

Variable overhead costs are

Indirect materials	$0.20 per unit
Indirect labor	$0.15 per unit
Other	$0.35 per unit

Fixed overheads costs for each quarter are

Salaries	14,000.00
Rent	11,000.00
Depreciation	8,082.50

You are required to:

1. Prepare a direct material purchased budget for Smith Chocolate

2. Prepare a direct labor cost budget for Smith Chocolate

3. Prepare a manufacturing overhead budget for Smith Chocolate

1.
Figure 3.43 Direct material purchased budget for this coming fiscal year, ending December 31

	Q1	Q2	Q3	Q4	Year
Units to be produced	40,800	49,200	59,200	51,300	200,500
Materials required per unit	× 1.5	× 1.5	× 1.5	× 1.5	× 1.5
Material needed in production(pounds)	61,200	73,800	88,800	76,950	300,750
Desired ending inventory	22,140	26,640	23,085	20,500	20,500
Materials needed in inventory	83,340	100,440	111,885	97,450	321,250
Desired opening inventory	-18,360	-22,140	-26,640	-23,085	-18,360
Direct materials to be purchased(pounds)	64,980	78,300	85,245	74,365	302,890
Cost of materials per pounds	× $2	× $2	× $2	× $2	× $2
Cost of direct materials to be purchased	$129,960	$156,600	$170,490	$148,730	$605,780

Direct material cost per unit = $605,780/200,500
= $3.02
= $3

2.
Figure 3.44 Direct Labor Cost Budget for this coming fiscal year, ending December 31

	Q1	Q2	Q3	Q4	Year
Units to be produced	40,800	49,200	59,200	51,300	200,500
labor hour/unit	× 0.2	× 0.2	× 0.2	× 0.2	× 0.2
Expected hours	8,160	9,840	11,840	10,260	40,100
Cost per hour	× $12	× $12	×	× $12	× $12

				$12	
Direct labor cost budget	$97,920	$118,080	$142,080	$123,120	$481,200

$$\text{Direct labor cost per unit} = \$481,200/200,500 = \$2.4$$

3.

Figure 3.45 Manufacturing overhead budget

	Q1	Q2	Q3	Q4	Year
Units to be produced	40,800	49,200	59,200	51,300	200,500
	$	$	$	$	$
Variable Overhead costs					
Indirect materials ($0.2 per unit)	8,160	9,840	11,840	10,260	40,100
Indirect labor ($0.15)	6,120	7,380	8,880	7,695	30,075
Other ($0.35 per unit)	14,280	17,220	20,720	17,955	70,175
Total variable overhead costs	28,560	34,440	41,440	35,910	140,350
Fixed overhead costs					
Salaries	14,000	14,000	14,000	14,000	56,000
Rent	11,000	11,000	11,000	11,000	44,000
Depreciation	8,083	8,083	8,083	8,083	32,330
Total Fixed overhead costs	33,083	33,083	33,083	33,083	132,330
Total overhead costs	61,643	67,523	74,523	68,993	272,680
Deduct Depreciation					

	(8,083)	(8,083)	(8,083)	(8,083)	(32,330)
Cash payment for overhead	53,560	59,440	66,440	60,910	240,350

Manufacturing overhead cost per unit
= $272,680/200,500

= $1.36

Illustration 3

Smith Chocolate, the company featured in the last illustration and in the next 2, is now preparing a selling and administrative budget, and income statement budget.

Assume smith chocolate estimates that all selling and administrative costs are fixed. Quarterly selling and administrative cost estimates for the coming year are:

Salaries	$30,000
Rent	$3,500
Advertisement	$5,000
Depreciation	$4,000
other	$500

You are required to prepare:
1. A selling and administrative budget for smith chocolate.
2. Prepare income statement budget for smith chocolate.

Solution

Smith Chocolate

Figure 3.46 Selling and Administrative Budget for this coming fiscal year, ending December 31

	Q1	Q2	Q3	Q4	Year

	$	$	$	$	$
Salaries	30,000	30,000	30,000	30,000	120,000
Rent	3,500	3,500	3,500	3,500	14,000
Advertisement	5,000	5,000	5,000	5,000	20,000
Depreciation	4,000	4,000	4,000	4,000	16,000
Other	500	500	500	500	2,000
Total selling and admin. Cost	43,000	43,000	43,000	43,000	172,000
Deduct depreciation	(4,000)	(4,000)	(4,000)	(4,000)	(16,000)
Cash payment for selling and admin.	39,000	39,000	39,000	39,000	156,000

Figure 3.47   Income Statement Budget for this coming fiscal year, ending December 31

	Q1 $	Q2 $	Q3 $	Q4 $	Year $
Sales	320,000	384,000	480,000	416,000	1,600,000
Cost of sales	(270,400)	(324,480)	(405,600)	(351,520)	(1,352,000)
Gross profit	49,600	59,520	74,400	64,480	248,000
Selling and Admin.	(43,000)	(43,000)	(43,000)	(43,000)	(172,000)
Net profit	6,600	16,520	31,400	21,480	76,000

Per unit cost of goods sold

	Year $
Direct materials (from Direct materials purchase budget)	3
Direct labor (from direct labor budget)	2.4
Manufacturing overhead (from manufacturing overhead budget)	1.36

Cost of goods sold per unit   6.76

Note:

The first line in the budgeted income statement; sales, comes from the sales budget in figure 3.41. The next line; cost of sales, is calculated by multiplying unit of sales in each quarter from figure 3.41. by $6.76

> Illustration 4
>
> Smith Chocolate has the following information pertaining to the capital expenditures and cash budgets.
>
> Capital Expenditures
>
> The company plans to purchase computer systems totaling $10,000 and production equipment totaling $14,000. Both will be purchased at the end of the fourth quarter and will not affect depreciation expenses for the coming year.
>
> Cash Budget
>
> All sales are on credit. The company expects to collect 70 percent of sales in the quarter of sales, 25 percent of sales in the quarter following the sales, and 5 percent will not be collected (bad debt). Accounts receivable at the end of last year totaled $100,000, all of which will be collected in the first quarter of this coming year.

All direct materials purchased are on credit. The company expects to pay 80 percent of purchases in the quarter of purchase and 20 percent the following quarter. Accounts payable at the end of last year totaled $25,000, all of which will be paid in the first quarter of this coming year.

The cash balance at the end of last year totaled $10,000.

Figure 3.48 Capital Expenditure Budget for this coming fiscal year, ending December 31

	Q1 $	Q2 $	Q3 $	Q4 $	Year $
Computer Systems	-	-	-	10,000	10,000
Production Equipment	-	-	-	14,000	14,000
Total				24,000	24,000

Figure 3.49 Cash Budget for this coming fiscal year, ending December 31

Cash collections from sales	Q1 $	Q2 $	Q3 $	Q4 $	Year $
Fourth quarter prior year	100,000				100,000
First quarter sales ($320,000)	224,000	80,000			304,000
Second quarter sales ($384,000)		268,800	96,000		364,800
Third quarter sales ($480,000)			336,000	120,000	456,000
Fourth quarter sales ($416,000)				291,200	291,200
	324,000	348,800	432,000	411,200	1,516,000

Cash payment for

purchases

of raw materials

Fourth quarter prior year	(25,000)				(25,000)
First quarter purchases ($129,960)	(103,968)	(25,992)			(129,960)
Second quarter purchases($156,600)		(125,280)	(31,320)		(156,600)
Third quarter purchases($170,490)			(136,392)	(34,098)	(170,490)
Fourth quarter purchases ($148,730)				(118,984)	(118,984)
Total cash payment for purchases	(128,968)	(151,272)	(167,712)	(153,082)	(601,034)
	(128,968)	(151,272)	(167,712)	(153,082)	(601,034)
Other cash payments					
Direct labor	(97,920)	(118,080)	(142,080)	(123,120)	(481,200)
Manufacturing overhead	(53,560)	(59,440)	(66,440)	(60,910)	(240,350)
Selling & Admin.	(39,000)	(39,000)	(39,000)	(39,000)	(156,000)
Capital Expenditure				(24,000)	(24,000)
Total other cash payment	(190,480)	(216,520)	(247,520)	(247,030)	(901,550)
Excess/shortage of collection over payments	4,552	(18,992)	16,768	11,088	13,416
Beginning cash balance	10,000	14,552	(4,440)	12,328	10,000
Ending cash balance	14,552	(4,440)	12,328	23,416	23,416

Illustration 5

Assume Smith Chocolate will collect 25 percent of fourth quarter budgeted sales in full next year (this represents accounts receivable at the end of the fourth quarter).

The following account balances are expected at the end of the fourth quarter:

Property, plant, and equipment (net) : $160,000
Common Stock   : $ 225,000

Retained earnings at the end of last year totaled $28,090 and no cash dividends are anticipated for the budget period ending December 31.

Prepare a budgeted balance sheet for Smith Chocolate.

Figure 3.50

Balance Sheet Budget for this coming fiscal year, December 31.

	$	$
Non-current Assets		
Property, Plant & Equipment(net)		160,000
Current Assets		
Inventory - Finished goods	30,420	
Inventory - Raw materials	41,000	
Accounts Receivable	104,000	
Cash Balance	23,416	
	198,836	198,836
Total assets		358,836
Current Liabilities		
Accounts payable		29,746
Shareholders' Equity		
Common Stock	225,000	
Retained earnings	104,090	

	329,090	329,090
Total liabilities and shareholders' equity		358,836

Notes:

Finished goods inventory:

$30,420 = 4,500 units (from production budget) x $6.76 cost per unit (from budgeted income statement)

Raw material Inventory:
$41,000 = 20,500 pounds x $2 per pound (from direct material budget)

Accounts Receivable:

$104,000 = $416,000 in budgeted fourth quarter sales x 25 percent to be collected next quarter

Accounts payable:

$29,746 = $148,730 in fourth quarter purchases (from direct materials budget) x 20 percent to be paid next quarter.

Retained earnings:

$104,090 = $28,090 in retained earnings end of last year + $76,000 budgeted net income (from budgeted income statements)

4. The whole or each item of income statement and statement of financial position for previous accounting period can be adjusted by a percentage increase or decrease to produce a Master budget for next accounting period. This method is common in accounting software.

For example, all items of statement of income for last year accounting period can be increased by 20% or decreased by 10%. Different percentages can also be used to adjust each of these items. The choice of adjustment should be the one that would produce a realistic and best result. It means that all items of statement of income for last year are adjusted by some specific percentages to produce the budget for this coming fiscal year.

5. You can also create an abstract income statement and statement of financial position and then adjust the values to produce budget for next accounting period. This is suitable for a business that just commences operation.

3.5 Cash Flow Budget or Cash Budget: This is a kind of budget that shows the expected cash inflow (receipts) and cash outflow (payments). It can also be called cash flow projection. Cash Flow Budget is used to determine when it is appropriate to borrow money or the appropriate time to invest your funds. When you prepare your cash flow budget and you discover that your cash outflow is higher than your cash inflow; you can borrow loan to finance the deficit, but when the cash inflow is greater than cash outflow; you can invest the surplus to generate income in the future.

Prepare cash flow budget for futures, such as next year, next quarter, next month and if your business is financially shaky, next week. An accurate cash flow projection can alert you of trouble before it strikes. This will make you to take necessary action in order to prevent the problem.

Cash flow projection must not be treated with frivolity. It is not a glimpse into the future. They are professional and educated guesses that consider a number of factors, including your customers' payment histories, your own research at identifying upcoming expenditures, and your vendors' patience.

There must be an assumption that cash inflows will continue to follow the same trend as they have recently and cash outflow will follow the same trend as they were occurring in the past, and that you have accounted for seasonal sales variation. The past and present performances of cash inflow and cash outflow can be used to predict cash flow for the future.

Start your cash flow projection by adding money on hand at the beginning of the period with other cash inflow during the period and deduct cash outflow for the period under consideration; the end result will be the cash flow projection for a particular period.

3.5.1 Benefits of Cash Flow Projection

The benefits to be derived from the preparation of cash flow projection are as follows:

(i) It provides early signal of potential cash deficit or cash surplus in order to take appropriate action.

(ii) It enables financial feasibility or plans to be ascertained.

(iii) It indicates the financial effects of policies within a firm.

(iv) It provides a base for monitoring actual activity. The frequent comparison of actual cash flow will enable up to date information to be incorporated into budget revisions.

3.5.2 Management of Cash Flow Deficit

A cash flow deficit arises when cash outflow is higher than cash inflow in a particular period. Cash flow deficit is also a situation in which a company is unable to pay its financial obligation as at when due because of insufficient cash balance.

Again, one of the purposes of cash flow projection is to enable an organization to know when an additional capital will be needed to be introduced into the business.

If you prepare your cash flow projection and you arrive at cash flow deficit, you don't need to be worry because you still have ample time at present to take necessary action before the deficit occurs. Some of the action to be taken to address cash flow deficit are as follows:

(i) Line credit

(ii) Short-term loan

(iii) Speed up the date of collecting accounts receivable

(iv) Delay the payment of accounts payable

(v) Liquidate investment

(vi) Cut expenses

The following are the explanations of the ways to address cash flow deficit:

Line credit: Use or spend above your credit card value. The amount to be spent above your credit card is limited by the regulation of your bank.

Short-term loan: You may apply for a short-term loan in order to cushion the cash flow deficit. There are some non-profit organizations that do not charge interest or that charge lower interest. You can patronize these organizations to obtain loans.

Speed up the rate of collecting accounts receivable: You may speed up the rate at which you recover money from your debtors. Ensure that debtors pay earlier than before. If the money is quickly collected from debtors, it can be used to cushion the cash flow deficit.

Cut Expenses: Ensure that you reduce your overhead expenses. Those expenses that can be reduced without any serious adverse effect on your business should be reduced.

Prioritize your expenditures: arrange your expenditures in order of priority. Meet those expenses according to their priority or importance so that most important expenses would have been paid for before cash deficit.

Liquidate Investment: You may liquidate some of your short-term investments. Some short-term investments such as treasury bills or treasury certificates may be liquidated in order to use the cash realized from it to cushion the effect of cash flow deficit.

Delay the payment of accounts payable: The payment to creditors or vendors may be delayed if it is possible. If the payment is delayed, the cash meant for the payment may be used to reduce cash flow deficit.

3.5.3   Management of cash Flow Surplus

Cash flow surplus occurs when cash inflow is greater than cash outflow in a particular period. It arises when you have more than enough cash to meet your financial obligation.

The following are the ways to manage your cash flow surplus:

Invest in short-term instruments: Your cash surplus should not be held idle. It must be used to do something that will eventually benefit your business. When you invest cash surplus in short-term investment you will receive interest. The short-term investment is also advantageous in the sense that it is a low risk-investment.

Increase your Accounts Receivable: You may increase your credit sales to only credible and credit worthy customers. By doing this, you are devising methods of wining and retaining customers for life.

Pay your Suppliers Earlier: You may pay some suppliers earlier from the cash surplus in order to enjoy the benefits of cash discounts. If you pay some suppliers earlier than the due date, they may also increase your credit facilities. All these will further increase your cash inflow later.

3.5.4 Procedures for the Preparation of Cash Flow Projection

Your organizational method of preparing cash flow projection is determined by the nature of your business, but the procedures are the same for all organizations.

You can start by using your annual operating or statement of income budget as the starting point. The operating budget or statement of income budget might not be on cash basis. You have to make an anticipation of how much cash will be received (cash inflow) and how much cash would be spent (cash outflow).

You begin by identifying each month expected cash income, each month expected cash expenditure and arrive at each month cash flow.

If you want your cash flow projection to be effective, it must be updated at least monthly, if not weekly. For more explanation, study the illustration and the suggested solution below.

ILLUSTRATION

From the following data, prepare a cash flow projection for the first six months of 2005 for SHINE Industries Ltd:

(i) Budgeted profit and Loss Accounts for the period ended 30 June 2005.

	Jan $'000	Feb $'000	March $'000	April $'000	May $'000	June $'000
Sales	90	92	88	95	90	94
Less purchases	54	56	50	60	52	55
Gross profit	36	36	38	35	38	39
Less operating expenses :						
Selling Exp.	-10	-12	-13	-13	-16	-15
Distribution Exp.	-6	-4	-5	-7	-4	-5
Admin Exp.	-3	-4	-4	-2	-5	-3
Net profit	17	16	16	13	13	16

(ii) Sales for November and December 2004 were $85,000 and $90,000 respectively.

(iii) 40% would be in cash and 30% each would be payable in 30days and 60days.

(iv) Purchase for November and December 2004 were $48,000 and $50,000 respectively.

(v) 75% of purchases would be paid immediately, and the balance in two- month time.

(vi) Selling expenses are to be settled in two equal installments in 30 and 60 days. December 2004 expenses are $15,000.

(vii) Distribution expenses are payable one month in arrears while administration expenses are payable immediately.

(viii) Distribution expenses for December 2004 would be $5,000 while administrative expenses would be $8,000 for November 2004 and $9,000 for December 2004.

(ix) Balance in the bank as at 31 December 2004 is expected to be $28,000 overdrawn.

(x) The company intends to pay for the following:

- Company tax of $12,000 in February 2005
- A new generator costing $6,500 in march 2005
- Dividends of $12,000 in April 2005.

(xi) Some unserviceable vehicles would be sold in January 2005 for $8,000. Show all workings.

SUGGESTED SOLUTION
SHINE Industries Ltd

	Jan $'000	Feb $'000	March $'000	April $'000	May $'000	June $'000	Total $'000
Income:							
Sales	88.5	90.8	89.8	92	90.9	93.1	545.1
Disposal	8						8
Total	96.5	90.8	89.8	92	90.9	93.1	553.1
Expenditure							
Purchases	52.5	54.5	51	59	51.5	56.2	324.8
Generator			6.5				6.5
Dividend				20			20
Tax		12					12
Selling Exp.	7.5	12.5	11	12.5	13	14.5	71
Distribution Exp.	5	6	4	5	7	4	31
Admin. Exp.	3	4	4	2	5	3	21
Total	68	89	76.5	98.5	76.5	77.7	486.3

Net cash flow	28.5	1.8	13.3	-6.5	14.4	15.35	66.85
Opening balance	-28	0.5	2.3	15.6	9.1	23.5	23
Closing balance	0.5	2.3	15.6	9.1	23.5	38.85	89.85

WORKINGS

Sales	Nov.	Dec.	Jan.	Feb.	March	April	May	June
	$'000	$'000	$'000	$'000	$'000	$'000	$'000	$'000
Actual	85	90	90	92	88	95	90	94
40%	34	36	36	36.8	35.2	38	36	37.6
30%		25.5	27	27	27.6	26.4	28.5	27
30%			25.5	27	27	27.6	26.4	28.5
Total	34	61.5	88.5	90.8	89.8	92	90.9	93.1

Purchases	Nov.	Dec.	Jan.	Feb.	March	April	May	June
	$'000	$'000	$'000	$'000	$'000	$'000	$'000	$'000
Actual	48	50	54	56	50			
75%	36	37.5	40.5	42	37.5	45	39	41.3
25%			12	12.5	13.5	14	12.5	15
Total	36	37.5	52.5	54.5	51	59	51.5	56.3

Selling Expenses	Dec.	Jan.	Feb.	March	April	May	June
Actual	15	10	12	13	13	16	15
50%		7.5	5	6	6.5	6.5	3
50%			7.5	5	6	6.5	6.5
Total		7.5	12.5	11	12.5	13	9.5

CHAPTER 4

4.0 TECHNIQUES USED IN BUDGETING

Learning Objectives

In this chapter, readers should be able to know

(i) Planning, Programming, Budgeting System (PPBS)

(ii) Various techniques used in budgeting

(iii) Zero Based Budgeting

(iv) Flexible and Fixed Budgeting

(v) Activity Based Budgeting

Techniques used In Budgeting

4.1 Fixed and Flexible Budgets

A fixed budget is a budget which is designed to remain unchanged regardless of the volume of output or turnover attained. It is a single budget with no analysis of costs.

The CIMA defines a flexible budget as "a budget which is designed to change in accordance with the level of activity attained". Flexible budget is a budget which is designed to adjust the permitted cost of activity level to suit the level of activity actually attained. The process by which this is done is by separating cost (semi variable cost) into their fixed and variable elements so that the budget may be flexed according to the actual activity.

Flexible budgeting is used for control purposes. The expected cost is compared with the actual cost incurred at the actual activity level.

ILLUSTRATION 4-1

Hybrid Ltd makes a product and has an average production of 10,000units a month although this varies widely. The following extract from its production department shows a make-up of the budget and a month's actual results.

		Budget for Production Of 10,000units	Actual results for Jan. production 9,300
	$	$	$
Indirect Labor			
Fixed	6,000		
Variable $1/unit	10,000	16,000	15,800
Consumables (variable)		30,000	28,500
Variable overheads		40,000	36,400
Fixed overheads		25,000	25,000
		111,000	105,700

You are required to show two budgetary control statements for January, one based on the fixed budget for 10,000units and one based on a flexible budget for the actual level of production.

Solution 1

Budgetary Control Statement 1

Fixed Budget Vs Actual Budget

Expense type	Fixed Budget 10,000 $	Actual results 9,300 $	Budget variance $
Indirect labor	16,000	15,800	200F
Consumables	30,000	28,500	1,500F
Variable o/h	40,000	36,400	3,600F
Fixed o/h	25,000	25,000	
	111,000	105,700	5,300F

Notes
(a) The variances are the differences between budgeted result and actual result. When budgeted cost is higher than the actual cost, the variance is said be favorable, but when the budgeted cost is lower than the actual cost, the variance is said to be adverse. In our solution above, the favorable variance is denoted by "F" while adverse variance is denoted by "A".

(b) When as in the case above, a planned activity level is different from the actual level of activity, the comparison of actual result with a fixed budget shows little or no meaningful information.

We can see in the solution above that the budgeted activity level is higher than the actual activity level and so is the total cost of budgeted activity level higher than the total cost of the actual activity level. The favorable variance may be as a result of inequality in the two activity levels being compared. In a nutshell, two equal activity levels; both budgeted activity level and actual activity level should be compared in order to arrive at meaningful information. Fixed budget fails to meet up with this criterion and hence is not appropriate for comparison of results.

Solution 2

Budgetary Control Statement based on Flexible Budget

		Flexible budget 9,300units	Actual Result 9,300units	Variance
Indirect labor	$	$	$	$
Fixed	6,000			
Variable($1/unit)	9,300	15,300	15,800	500A
Consumables($3/unit)		27,900	28,500	600A
Variable o/h ($4/unit)		37,200	36,400	800F
Fixed o/h		25,000	25,000	
		105,400	105,700	300A

Workings

1. Indirect labor cost(variable):
   = $10,000

$$\frac{10{,}000}{} = \$1/\text{unit}$$

2. Consumables (all variable):
$$= \frac{\$30{,}000}{10{,}000} = \$3/\text{unit}$$

3. Variable overhead:
$$= \frac{\$40{,}000}{10{,}000} = \$4/\text{unit}$$

4. Fixed cost remains unchanged regardless of the changes in the level of activity.

NOTE:

As stated in the definition of flexible budget; all budgeted costs change except fixed cost in accordance with the level of activity attained.

In order to know cost that changes and cost that remains unchanged, semi-variable costs need to be separated into its variable and fixed elements.

ILLUSTRATION 4-2

Samotex Limited is operating a system of flexible Budgetary Control.

Her budgets for the year are as follows:

	70%	80%	90%	100%
	units	units	units	units

	700 $	800 $	900 $	1000 $
Prime costs	14,000	16,000	18,000	20,000
Variable overhead (production)	2,100	2,400	2,700	3,000
Semi-variable overhead selling:				
Distribution	3,400	3,600	3,800	4,000
Other fixed overhead	3,000	5,000	5,000	5,000
Total	22,500	27,000	29,500	32,000

You are required to present the above to the management, separating semi-variable into variable and fixed overhead and also include the cost of "attaining 120% level of activity". Fixed cost remains unchanged.

SOLUTION 4-2

Budgetary Statement based on Flexible budget

	70% units 700 $	80% units 800 $	90% units 900 $	100% Units 1,000 $	120% units 1,200 $
Prime costs	14,000	16,000	18,000	20,000	24,000
Variable overhead (production)	2,100	2,400	2,700	3,000	3,600

	16,100	18,400	20,700	23,000	27,600
Variable overhead selling & distribution	1,400	1,600	1,800	2,000	2,400
Total variable cost	17,500	20,000	22,500	25,000	30,000
Fixed cost	7,000	7,000	7,000	7,000	7,000
Total cost	24,500	27,000	29,500	32,000	37,000

WORKINGS

Variable cost per unit = Highest cost - Lowest cost
$\qquad\qquad\qquad\qquad\qquad\,\,$ Highest units - Lowest units

Prime cost = $20,000 - $14,000
$\qquad\qquad\,\,$ 1,000 – 700
$\qquad\,\,$ = 6,000/300
$\qquad\,\,$ = $20

Variable overhead (production) = 3,000 - 2,100
$\qquad\qquad\qquad\qquad\qquad\qquad$ 1,000 – 700
$\qquad\qquad\qquad\qquad\qquad\,$ = 900/300
$\qquad\qquad\qquad\qquad\qquad\,$ = $3

There are different methods for the separation of semi-variable costs into variable and fixed elements. High and Low method is prescribed here.

Classification of semi- variable overhead selling and distribution into its variable and fixed elements using high and low method are as follows:

Variable cost per unit = Highest cost - Lowest cost
$\qquad\qquad\qquad\qquad\qquad\,\,$ Highest units - Lowest units

variable overhead selling & distribution = $\frac{4{,}000 - 3{,}400}{1{,}000 - 700}$

= 600/300

= $2

Fixed overhead selling & distribution:

$y = a + bx$

$4,000 = a + 2 × $1,000

$4,000 = a + $2,000

-a = $2,000 - $4,000

-a = - $2,000

a = $2,000

NOTE:

It should be noted that when semi-variable overhead is separated into fixed overhead and variable overhead, the fixed overhead is $2,000 while variable overhead per unit is $2. It should be emphasized that total fixed cost is constant but total variable cost is not constant. Variable cost per unit is constant.

Fixed overhead selling & distribution is $2,000. This fixed cost remains unchanged irrespective of the level of activity or output.

If the fixed overhead selling & distribution is deducted from each of the semi-variable overhead selling and distribution under each level of activity, variable overhead selling and distribution is the amount that remains in each case.

4.2 Zero Based Budgeting (ZBB)

ZBB is a cost-benefit approach where it is assumed that the cost allowance for an item is zero, and will remain so until the manager responsible justifies the existence of the cost item and the benefits the expenditure brings. ZBB can also be referred to as priority based budgeting.

Zero based budgeting is "a method of budgeting which requires each cost element to be specifically justified, as though, the budgets related were being undertaken for the first time, without approval, the budget allowance is zero" CIMA.

4.2.1. The use of ZBB was pioneered by P. Phyrr in the United States in the early 1970, and has gained wide acceptance and prominence because of the fact that it is based on common sense. President Carter, the president of the United States, directed all United States government departments to adopt this technique. ZBB is concerned with the evaluation of the cost and benefits of alternative, and implicit in the technique; is the concept of opportunity cost.

4.2.2 Where can ZBB be applied?

ZBB can be applied in both profit making and non profit making organization.

4.2.3 Stages in Implementing ZBB

The overall process of implementing a ZBB system can be sub-divided into three stages thus:

a) The decision units: This means subdividing the organization to discrete sub-units where operations can be meaningfully and individually identified and evaluated.

b) The decision Packages: Each decision unit manager submits no less than three budget packages namely (i) the lowest level of expenditure (ii) the expenditure required to maintain levels of activity (iii) the expenditure required to provide an additional level of service or activity.

c) Agreed packages will form the budget.

4.2.4 Advantages and Disadvantages of ZBB

Advantages of ZBB

(i) It focuses attention on value for money
(ii) Managers performance can be monitored
(iii) It results in a more efficient allocation of resources to activities and departments.
(iv) It may result in cost reduction

Disadvantages of ZBB

(i) ZBB is a time consuming process and generates volume of paperwork especially for the decision packages.
(ii) Co-ordination of all activities may be difficult.
(iii) Trade unions always go against ZBB, who prefer status quo to remain.

4.3 Activity Based Budgeting (ABB)

Activity Based Budgeting (ABB) which is also known as Activity Cost Management is defined as "a method of budgeting based on an activity framework and utilizing cost driver data in the budget setting and variance feed back process". (CIMA)

It is a development of conventional budgeting systems and is based on activity analysis techniques.

4.3.1 Features of ABB

a. It recognises activities which drive costs with the aim of controlling the causes of cost directly rather than the costs themselves. In the long-run, costs will be managed and better understood.
b. It recognises that not all activities add value so it is essential to differentiate and examine activities for their value adding potential.
c. It recognises that majority of activities in a department are driven by demands and decisions which are beyond the control of budget holder.
d. It encourages immediate and relevant performance measures required more than are found in conventional budgeting systems.

4.3.2 Advantages of ABB

1. It uses activity analysis techniques which promotes continuous improvement.
2. It has ability to tackle cross organizational issues through a participating approach.

4.4 Planning, Programming, Budgeting System (PPBS)

PPBS analyses the output of a given program and also seeks for the alternatives to find the most effective means of reaching basic program activities.

PPBS involve the preparation of a long-term corporate plan that clearly establishes the objective that the organization intends to achieve.

4.4.1 Aims and objectives of PPBS

(i) It enables the management to identify activities, functions or programs to be provided thereby establishing a basis for evaluation of their worthiness.
(ii) PPBS provide information that will enable management to assess the effectiveness of its plans.

4.4.2 Stages in PPBS

The following are the stages involved in PPBS

(i) Calls for a careful specification and overall objectives are determined.
(ii) Identify programs that will achieve these objectives and those programs which are normally related to

4.5 Continuous Budget/Rolling Budget

Continuous budget which is known as rolling budget is a system of budgeting that involves continuously updating budgets by reviewing the actual results of a specific period in the budget and determining a budget for the corresponding time period.

CHAPTER 5

FORCASTING AND BUDGETARY CONTROL

Learning Objectives

In this chapter, readers should be able to:

(i) Differentiate between Budgeting and Budgetary control.

(ii) Explain Forecast and Budget

(iii) Know Forecasting procedures

Forecasting and Budgetary Control

5.1 Difference between Forecast and Budget

A forecast states the events which are likely to occur in the future. To forecast is to predict. A budget states the plans which the managers will endeavor to turn into actual events. It is a statutory executive order.

5.1.1 Forecasting Procedures

Forecasting can be applied in many sections or departments of an organization. The most important department in which forecast can be applied is sales department.

There are many approaches to arrive at the sales forecasts. Some of the ways are explained below:

1. Assessment by staff of sales department: Estimates should be made by the individual salesmen and transferred upwards to the sales manager. This is beneficial to the company because the individual salespersons know much about what happens within the sales department.

2. Senior Management Decision: The senior management team, including production manager, administrative manager etc., will come together to discuss sales prospects. The approach brings a variety of skills and experiences to the forecasting exercise.

3. Mathematical analysis of past sales: Such analysis should indicate trends and seasonal variations. The information can be adjusted for known factor like increasing advertisement, to give a forecast of future sales.

The sales budget will be determined by reference to the sales forecast. However, the budget should be prepared in the light of any limiting factor or constraints on the amount that can be produced.

5.1.2 Budgetary Control

There is a significant difference between a budget and budgetary control/budgeting.

A budget is just an integral part of budgetary control/budgeting. Budgetary control is defined as a system of controlling costs which includes the preparation of budgets, coordinating the departments and establishing responsibilities, comparing actual performance with the budget and acting upon the results to achieve maximum profitability (CIMA).

Certain fundamental principles can be outlined from the above definition of budgetary control:

a) Establish a plan or target of performance which co-ordinates all the activities of the business;
b) Record the actual performance;
c) Compare the actual performance with the plan or target of performance
d) Calculate the differences or variances, and analysis the reasons for them; and
e) Act immediately, if necessary, to remedy the situation.

5.1.3 Objectives of Budgetary Control

The following are the objectives of budgetary control:

a) To combine the ideas of all levels of management in the preparation of the budget;

b) To co-ordinate all activities of the business;

c) To centralize Control;

d) To act as a guide for management decisions;

e) To plan and control income and expenditure so that maximum profitability is achieved;

f) To direct capital expenditure in the most profitable direction;

g) To ensure that sufficient working capital is available for the efficient operation of the business;

h) To provide a benchmark against which actual activity can be compared;

i) To show management which action is needed to correct situation.

5.1.4 Procedures and Organization for Budgetary Control

Procedures and Organization for budgetary control are as follows:

1) The preparation of an organizational chart: This enables each member of management to know his or her functional responsibility and position in the company and his or her relationship with other members.

2) Budget period is the time to which a plan of activity relates. Budget period cover a specific period of time commonly a year. They will be divided into shorter time periods (sub-periods) known as: control periods, for purpose of reporting control. In a one-year period budget, control period may be monthly (12 periods each year), or quarterly (4 periods each year). Long term budget can be for a period of 3years or more. Example of long-term budget is capital expenditure budgets.

3) Budget Manual: The organization for budgeting and budgeting control should be documented in a budget manual. Budget manual has been already explained earlier in this book.

4) Budget Committee: The overall responsibility for budget preparation and administration should be given to a Budget Committee.

5) The Budget officer: A budget officer controls the administration of budget. He co-ordinate all the functional budgets. He prepares the master budget and cash flow budget.

6) Budget Center: A business entity's planned activities are divided into separate areas known as budget canters or cost centers. A separate budget is prepared for each budget centre. A budget centre is known as a departmental or a functional budget.

7) Limiting Factor or Key Factor or Principal Budget Factor: Limiting factor is that factor that limits the activity of an organization. It may be customers' demand, production capacity, Shortage of materials, labor, space or finance. Limiting factor should be identified and its effect on each of the budgets carefully considered during the budget preparation process.

8) Level of Activity: This is the normal level of activity expected to be attained by a company. It includes quantity to produce, quantity to be sold, etc.

9) Control: The process of comparing actual result with the planned result and reporting on the variation; is the principle of budgetary control. It helps to keep expenditure within agreed limit.

CHAPTER 6

CAPITAL EXPENDITURE PLANNING AND CONTROL

In this chapter, readers should be able to understand:

(i) Capital Expenditure planning.

(ii) Capital budgeting procedures.

6.1.1. INTRODUCTION

Capital expenditures are the expenditures incurred on the acquisition of fixed assets and other long-term projects to generate future flow of economic benefits. In this context, capital expenditure is regarded as a capital investment. These capital expenditures require huge amount of money, and hence all efforts should be taken to plan and control capital expenditure in order to avoid wasteful spending.

There are cases when the equipment is the major asset that generates income for a company. For example, the aircraft and the ship are the backbone of an airline and shipping company, respectively.

The capital expenditure has to be properly planned, evaluated and controlled.

The future cash flows (economic benefits) have to be properly estimated, and this is the most difficult aspect of the planning and evaluation process. When the company concern has appropriately estimated the future cash flows of each capital investment available, the evaluation of each investment proposal using appropriate investment techniques is the next. Each investment proposal should be evaluated based on its capacity and ability to achieve minimum expected return by the providers of capital.

6.2 Capital Investment Decision or Capital Expenditure planning and Control

Pandy(1989 defined capital expenditure planning and control as "a process of facilitating decision covering expenditure on long-term assets".

Capital expenditure planning and control is an integral part of the corporate planning of an organisation. It is also called **capital budgeting** or **capital investment decision**.

Capital budgeting process includes:

i) Identification of investment opportunities

ii) Developing cash flow estimation

iii) Evaluation of the net benefits

iv) Authorization to spend

v) Control and monitoring of capital projects

i. Identification of investment opportunities

Investment proposals should be properly identified because once fund is committed on it, it cannot be reversed. An effective investment appraisal technique which should maximise the shareholders' wealth should be used to measure the economic worth of projects.

ii. Development of cash flow estimation

Estimation of cash flow for the future has to be developed but the future is uncertain. As a result of this uncertainty of the future, development and forecasting of cash flow might be difficult. It is therefore, important to take action necessary to arrive at reliable cash flows.

iii. Evaluation of the net benefits

The method or investment appraisal that will reveal the appropriate or investment appraisal with highest net benefits should be adopted. This means that whatever criterion that is applied should be capable of ranking projects correctly in terms of profitability.

At minimum, the benefits from the investment selected must be higher than its cost adjusted for time value and risk.

In this particular case, the net present value method is theoretically recommended, among others by experts as it has a true measure of profitability. It ranks projects correctly and is consistent with the wealth maximization criterion. However, other methods in use aside Net Present Value (NPV), are the payback period, the Internal Rate of Return (IRR), Accounting Rate of Return, and Profitability Index (PI).

In the implementation of a sophisticated evaluation system, The use of minimum required rate of return is necessary. This should be based on the riskiness of cash flows of the investment proposed which are considered to be commonly influenced by the following factors, amongst others:

i. Inflation

ii. Government policies

iii. Project life

iv. Product demand

v. Price of raw materials and other inputs

There are some capital budget techniques that are suggested to take care of risks. Some of these include:

1) Simulation techniques

2) Sensitivity analysis
3) Conservative analysis
4) Conservative forecasts
5) Standard Deviation
6) Co-efficient of variation

iv. Authorization to Spend

The approval to incur capital expenditure depends on the peculiarity of each company's organisational chart. However, when huge capital expenditure is involved, the authority for the final approval may rest with the board of directors or the top management level.

The approval authority may be delegated to junior management for certain types of investment projects involving small amounts of capital. Funds are usually appropriated for capital expenditure from the capital budget after the final selection of investment appraisal.

v. Control and Monitoring of capital projects

A capital project reporting system is required to review and monitor the performance of investment projects before and after the completion. This will make it easy to compare actual performance with original estimates.

CHAPTER 7

INVESTMENT APPRAISAL TECHNIQUES

In this chapter, readers will be able to understand:

(i) Investment appraisal Techniques

(ii) Different situations of investment appraisal

Investment Appraisal Techniques

There are many methods for selecting investments in long-term assets (capital expenditure). The methods of selecting investments in capital expenditures are called investment appraisal techniques.

The investment appraisal technique which is capable of producing the most valid technique of evaluating investment in a project should be selected and used for the evaluation of investment, or investment technique that will evaluate investment in accordance with the objective of the shareholder's wealth maximization should be selected.

Investment appraisal techniques can be used in two scenarios.

They are as follows:

1. Investment appraisal techniques under certainty
2. Investment appraisal techniques under uncertainty and risks.

It is necessary to accentuate that expenditure incurred on investment and benefits expected from an investment should be measured in cash. In this regard, it is the cash flow that is important and not the accounting profit.

Assumptions of Investment Appraisal

The following are the assumptions of investment appraisal:

i. It is assumed that the opportunity cost (rate of return) of capital project is known.

ii. it is assumed that the cost of investment or the amount of capital expenditure on investment is known.

iii. The benefits or cash flow from the investments are known.

7.1. Investment Appraisal Techniques under Certainty

Investment appraisal techniques under certainty are the capital budgeting techniques that are used to assess projects' viability when the outcome of the projects can be predict with certainty.

Investment appraisal which is also called capital budgeting can be evaluated using various techniques. The capital budgeting techniques under certainty can be grouped into two. They are as follows:

1. Non-Discounted Cash Flow Techniques

a. Payback Period
b. Accounting Rate of Return (ARR)

2. Discounted Cash Flow Techniques

a. Net Present Value (NPV)
b. Internal rate of Return
c. Profitability Index
d. Discounted payback period

CHAPTER 8

NON-DISCOUNTED CASH FLOW TECHNIQUES

Learning Objectives

After studying this chapter, you should be able to:

(i) Evaluate capital projects using Pay Back Period Technique.

(ii) Evaluate capital project using Accounting Rate of Return (ARR) technique.

Non-Discounted Cash Flow Techniques

a)   Payback Period

This technique pays attention to the shortness of the project; it means the shorter the period of recovery of initial investment or capital outlay, the more acceptable the project becomes. It shows the number of years in which the initial investment will be recovered from the cash inflows of the investment.

CIMA defines payback period as the period usually expressed in years, in which the cash outflows will equate the cash inflows from a project.

Decision rule

If the payback period calculated for a period is less than the standard payback period set by the management, the project would be accepted. If not, it would be rejected.

If mutually exclusive projects are involved, whereby only one of the projects can be undertaken, the rule is to accept the project with the shorter payback period.

Advantages of Payback Period

1) It is simple to calculate and understand
2) It is less exposed to uncertainty since it only focuses on shortness of a project
3) It is a fast screening techniques especially for the firms that have liquidity problems

Disadvantages of Payback Period
1) It does not take into consideration the time value of money
2) It does not take accounts of cash flow earned after the payback period.
3) It does not take into consideration the risks associated with each project.

ILLUSTRATION 1

Mr. Smith runs a manufacturing business. The project involves an immediate cash outlay of $20,000. He estimated that the net cash flows from the project will be as follows:

Years	Cash flow ($)
1	2,000
2	4,000
3	22,000
4	8,000

Calculate Mr. Smith payback period for the project. The company's required payback period is fixed at 2years and 5months.

Solution

Years	Cash flow ($)	Cumulative cash flow ($)
0	-20,000	-20,000
1	2,000	-18,000
2	4,000	-14,000
3	22,000	
4	8,000	

Procedures:

Deduct cash inflow for each year from the initial outlay (cash outflow) until the whole cash outflow has been exhausted.

Payback period = 2years + $\frac{14,000}{22,000}$ ×12 months

= 2years and 7.6 months

Decision rule

Using the payback period, accept project that has shorter payback period than the company's required payback period.

This project should be rejected because its payback period (2 years and 7.6 months) is higher that the company's set payback period (2years and 5months).

ILLUSTRATION 2

PZY Ltd, a manufacturing company, is faced with the problem of choosing between two mutually exclusively projects.

Project A requires a cash outlay of $25,000 and generates a net cash flow of $10,000 per year for 4 years.

Project B requires a cash outlay of $15,000 and generates net cash flow of $6,500, $5,500, $4,000, $5,000 over its life of 4 years.

Which one of the projects should be accepted?

Solution

Project A

Payback period = $\frac{\text{Initial outlay}}{\text{Annual Net Cash flow}}$

$$= \frac{\$25,000}{\$10,000}$$

$$= 2.5$$

$$= 2 \text{ years} + 0.5 \times 12 \text{months}$$

$$= 2 \text{ years and 6months}$$

Project B

Years	Cash flow ($)	Cumulative cash flow ($)
0	-15,000	-15,000
1	6,500	-8,500
2	5,500	-3,000
3	4,000	
4	5,000	

$$\text{Payback period} = 2 \text{ years} + \frac{3,000}{4,000}$$

$$= 2 + 0.75 \times 12 \text{months}$$

$$= 2 \text{years and 9months}$$

Decision:

Accept project A and reject project B because project A has earlier pay back period than project B.

b) **Accounting Rate of Return**

The accounting rate of return (ARR) is derived from the concept of return on capital employed (ROCE) or invested (ROI). It uses the accounting information provided by the financial statements to measure the profitability of an investment. The formula for the calculation of ARR is mentioned below:

$$ARR = \frac{\text{Average profit after tax}}{\text{Average investment}}$$

Note: Average profit after tax is the total profit after tax divided by number of years of the project.

Decision Rule:

The rule is to accept all projects that have higher Accounting Rate of Return than the company's predetermined rate.

Where mutually exclusive projects are involved, the rule is to accept the project that has highest ARR.

Advantages of Accounting Rate of Return

1. It is easy to calculate
2. It is easy to understand and use
3. it incorporates the entire stream of income in calculating projects' profitability.

Disadvantages of Accounting Rate of Return

1. The averaging of income ignores the time value of money.
2. It uses accounting profits in appraising the projects.
3. It does not take into consideration the risk associated with each project as well as the attitude of the management of the company to risk.

ILLUSTRATION 1

Otega recently convinced his friends and relations to grant him a loan of $100,000, which he intends to invest in a farming project. He estimates that the project will yield the following returns annually for next five consecutive years.

Years	$
1	30,000
2	30,000
3	40,000
4	30,000
5	20,000

There were no expectations of scrap values at the end of the fifth year and the project is to be evaluated using Accounting Rate of Return.

Note:

The company's predetermined minimum acceptable ARR is 68%.

You are required to provide the accounting rate of return for the project on the assumption that the annual returns are profits after tax.

Solution:

$$ARR = \frac{\text{Average profit after tax}}{\text{Average investment}} \times 100\%$$

Total annual investment:

$
30,000
30,000
40,000
30,000
<u>20,000</u>
150,000

Average profit after tax = $\dfrac{150{,}000}{5}$

$= \$30{,}000$

Average investment $= \$100{,}000/2$

$= \$50{,}000$

ARR $= \dfrac{\$30{,}000}{\$50{,}000} \times 100\%$

$= 0.6 \times 100\%$

$= 60\%$

Decision Rule:

a) The rule is to invest in all projects whose accounting rate of return are higher than the company's predetermined minimum Accounting Rate of Return.

b) Where there are mutually exclusive projects, the project that has highest ARR should be accepted.

From the solution above, the ARR calculated from the project above is 60%. This is lower than the company's predetermined minimum rate of return (68%). As a result of this, the project should be rejected because it generates lower ARR than the company's predetermined ARR.

CHAPTER 9

CONCEPTS IN CAPITAL BUDGETING DECISION

Learning Objectives

In this chapter, readers will be able to understand:

        (i) Concept of time value of money

        (ii) Concept of annuity

        (iii) Concept of perpetuity

        (iv) Concept of relevant cash flow

Concepts in Capital Budgeting Decision

In order to facilitate the understanding of two methods (that is, NPV and IRR) we shall explain some basic concepts as they apply to capital budgeting decisions. The concepts are the following:

a) Concept of time value of money

b) Concept of annuity

c) Concept of perpetuity

d) Concept of relevant cash flows

9.1. Concept of Time Value of Money

Time value of money states that an amount of money now will be greater than the same amount in the future. $1 today is greater than $1 in the future.

Where future value of an amount invested is given, what is the amount invested to generate the future value being given? That is, what is the present value of the future amount given?

In arriving at the present value of the future value, returns or interest on the money invested must be forgone.

This concept is based on compound interest formula.

$FV = PV(1+r)^n$

Where:

Fv = future value of money receivable in a period
Pv = principal or present value
r = the rate of interest or cost of capital
n = number of years

Pv can be made subject of the formula in the formula above.

$$Pv = \frac{Fv}{(1+r)^n}$$

$Pv = Fv(1+r)^{-n}$

Where $(1+r)^{-n}$ is the discount factor.

ILLUSTRATION

Calculate the present value of $10,000 receivable in 5 years time if the interest rate is 10%.

$$\begin{aligned}
Pv &= Fv(1+r)^{-n} \\
&= 10,000(1+0.1)^{-5} \\
&= \$10,000 \times 0.6209 \\
&= \$6,209
\end{aligned}$$

9.2. Concept of Annuity

An annuity is a constant sum of money receivable or payable over a specific period of time.

The present value of annuity can be calculated using the formula below:

$$Pv = \frac{A(1 - (1+r)^{-n})}{r}$$

Where:

Pv = Present value of annuity
A = The constant or equal annual sum
r = rate of interest or cost of capital
n = number of years

ILLUSTRATION

Calculate the present value of $1,000 receivable every year for 5 years at the interest rate of 10% per annum.

$$Pv = \frac{A(1 - (1+r)^{-n})}{r}$$

$$Pv = \frac{1,000 \times (1 - (1+0.1)^{-5})}{0.1}$$

$$= \frac{1,000 \times (1 - (1.1)^{-5})}{0.1}$$

$$= \$3,791$$

9.3. Concept of Perpetuity

Concept of Perpetuity is described as a situation in which constant sum of money is saved or withdrawn for an indefinite time. It can also be defined as a perpetual annuity.

The formula for calculating present value of perpetual annuity is described below:

$Pv = A \times 1/r$

Where:

Pv = Present value of annuity
A = The constant or equal annual sum
r = rate of interest or cost of capital

ILLUSTRATION

Calculate the present value of $1,000 receivable every year for indefinite period at the interest rate of 10% per annum.

$Pv = A \times 1/r$

$= \$1,000 \times 1/0.1$

$= \$10,000$

9.4. Relevant cash Flow

Where the present value is used, we state that the cash flows used are Discounted Cash flow. The discounted cash flow techniques namely the NPV and IRR used for evaluation of capital projects recognise only relevant cash flow of a project.

In order to assess a project properly, we need to determine the relevant costs and this is done by taking the following steps:

a) Determine the kind of decision to be taken, for example, accept or reject a project, abandon and replace a project line, scrap a product line, make or buy an item etc.

b) Any cash flow that will be influenced or affected by (a) above is relevant.

c) Do not focus your attention only on the project that is being evaluated but consider its effects on the other operations of the company. This is called opportunity cost concept which can be a function of cost or revenue thus:

i. If the decision will result in additional expenses or increased running costs in other operations of the company, then this cost must be included as relevant cash outflows in the original decision in (a) above

ii. Similarly, if the project being evaluated will result in additional contributions or savings from other operations of the company, then those savings must be treated as relevant cash inflows in the evaluation of decisions in (a) above.

d) The following are not relevant for projects' evaluation:
i. all appropriations, reserves and other non cash items.
ii. All fixed costs except incremental or attributable fixed costs
iii. All historical or sunk or past costs
iv. Cost of carrying out research and development

Additional Assumptions of capital budgeting are as follows:

i. The period in which capital or fund is invested should be tagged as year zero in any investment appraisal. It is always at the beginning of investments of year 1 or the first year and it is to be taken as a year on its own, that is year zero.

ii. All other cash flows after year zero are assumed to arise at the end of the year to which they relate.

CHAPTER 10

DISCOUNTED CASH FLOW TECHNIQUES

Learning Objectives

After studying this chapter, you should be able to:

      (i)   Distinguish between NPV and IRR

      (ii)   Evaluate capital projects using discounted cash flow techniques

      (iii)   Know IRR modification

Discounted Cash Flow Techniques

10.1. Net Present Value

Net present value is one of the discounted cash flow that emphasizes on time value of money. It is the net contribution of a project to its owners' wealth, that is, the present value of future cash flows minus the present value of initial capital investment.

All cash flows are discounted to their present value using the required rate of return under present value method. The formula for calculating NPV can be written as follows:

$$NPV = [C_1 \times (1+r)^{-1} + C_2 \times (1+r)^{-2} \ldots C_n \times (1+r)^{-n}] - C_0$$

C_1 C_2.... represent cash inflows in year 1, 2...n

r represents the opportunity cost of capital

C_0 is the initial cost of the investment

r represents the opportunity cost of capital

$(1+r)^{-n}$ is the discounting factor for each year

Advantages of NPV

(i) It recognises the time value of money

(ii) It includes all the cash flow involved in the entire life of a project in its calculation.

(iii) it is more useful than the IRR in decision under capital rationing i.e. shortage of investments funds

Disadvantages of NPV

(i) It is more difficult to calculate than PBP and ARR.

(ii) It relies heavily on the correct estimation of cost of capital i.e. where errors occur in the cost of capital used for discounting the decision, using the NPV would be misleading.

ILLUSTRATION 1

A machine costing $20,000 will provide annual net cash inflow of $6,000 for six years at a cost of capital of 10%.

You are required to:

  i. Calculate the net present value (NPV) of the machine

  ii. Should the machine be purchased?

   Solution

years	Cash flow ($)	DCF (10%)	PV ($)
0	-20,000	1	-20,000
1	6,000	0.9091	5,455
2	6,000	0.8265	4,959
3	6,000	0.7513	4,508
4	6,000	0.683	4,098
5	6,000	0.6209	3,725
6	6,000	0.5645	3,387
		NPV	6,132

(ii) Decision: The machine should be purchased because the NPV is positive, that is NPV > 0

Alternatively, annuity as earlier explained in the concept of annuity can also be used to discount the above cash flow and solve the question since the same amount ($6,000) is being expected throughout the years under consideration. The NPV of the project can be calculated as follow:

The discount factor from year 1 to 6 is

$$= \frac{1-(1+r)^{-n}}{r}$$

$$= \frac{1-(1+0.1)^{-6}}{0.1}$$

$$= 4.3553$$

Years	Cash flow($)	DCF (10%)	PV($)
0	-20,000	1	-20,000
1 to 6	6,000	4.3553	26,131.8
		NPV	6,132

NOTE:

Where constant cash flows are generated from a project, annuity formula (discount factor) should be used to discount the cash flows.

Decision Rule:

Accept all projects that produce positive Net Present value (NPV)

Accept if NPV > 0
Reject if NPV < 0
May accept or reject if NPV = 0

10.2. Internal Rate of Return (IRR)

The IRR is that cost of capital that will produce NPV of zero when applied to a project. It is a breakeven point cost of capital. It is also the cost of capital or discount rate that will equate the total cash outflow to the total cash inflow of a project.

In order to generate the cost of capital (IRR) that will produce Zero NPV, the following procedures may be followed:

a) Generate two (2) opposite values of NPV (+ and – value) using two different discount rates earlier calculated. It should be noted that the higher the discount rate, the lower the NPV and vice versa.

b) The above two opposite NPV and the two different discount rates may be applied in the formula below:

$$IRR = Lr + \frac{NPVLr}{NPVLr - (-NPVHr)} \times (Hr - Lr)$$

Where:

Lr = Lower rate of return
Hr = Higher rate of return
$NPVLr$ = Net present value of lower rate of return

NPVHr = Net present value of higher rate of return

Advantages of IRR

i. It recognizes time value of money

ii. It is consistent with shareholders' wealth maximization objective.

iii. It considers all cash flows occurring over the entire life of a project.

Disadvantages of IRR

i. It is more difficult to calculate than the other methods

ii. In some cases, it fails to indicate a correct choice between mutually exclusive projects.

iii. Sometimes, it yields multiple rates

iv. It can give misleading and inconsistent results when the NPV of a project does not decline with discount rates.

ILLUSTRATION 1

A machine costing $20,000 will provide annual net cash inflow of $6,000 for six years at a cost of capital of 10%. Calculate the Internal rate of Return of the machine

Solution

Step1: calculation of the rate that generates +NPV

years	Cash flow($)	DCF (10%)	PV ($)
0	-20,000	1	-20,000

1	6,000	0.9091		5,455
2	6,000	0.8265		4,959
3	6,000	0.7513		4,508
4	6,000	0.683		4,098
5	6,000	0.6209		3,725
6	6,000	0.5645		3,387
		NPV		6,132

Step 2: calculation of the rate that generates – NPV

Years	Cash flow ($)	DCF (20%)	PV ($)
0	-20,000	1	-20,000
1	6,000	0.8333	5,000
2	6,000	0.6944	4,166
3	6,000	0.5787	3,472
4	6,000	0.4823	2,894
5	6,000	0.4019	2,411
6	6,000	0.3349	2,009
		NPV	-47

The formula can then be applied here:

$$IRR = Lr + \frac{NPVLr}{NPVLr - (-NPVHr)} \times (Hr - Lr)$$

$$IRR = 10\% + \frac{6,132}{6,132 - (-47)} \times (20 - 10)\%$$

IRR = 19.92%

Decision Rule:

Accept all projects whose IRR are greater than the company's cost of capital.

i.e. Accept if r > k

Reject if r < k

May accept or reject if r = k

Where r = internal rate of return and k = cost of capital of the company

Where mutually exclusive projects are involved, the rule is to accept project that produces highest IRR.

10.3. Profitability Index

Profitability Index can be calculated using the following formula:

$$PI = \frac{NPV \text{ of a project}}{\text{Initial cash outlay}}$$

Or

$$PI = \frac{PV \text{ of cash inflow}}{\text{Initial outlay}}$$

Advantages of PI

i. It recognizes the time value of money

ii. It is generally consistent with wealth maximization principle

iii. It is a variation of the NPV method and requires the same computation as in the NPV method

Disadvantages of PI

i. It cannot be used to evaluate mutually exclusive projects or dependent projects.

ii. It can only be used under simple situation.

ILLUSTRATION 1

A machine costing $20,000 will provide annual net cash inflow of $6,000 for six years at a cost of capital of 10%. Calculate profitability index of the project.

Solution

years	Cash flow($)	DCF(10%)	PV ($)
0	-20,000	1	-20,000
1	6,000	0.9091	5,455
2	6,000	0.8265	4,959
3	6,000	0.7513	4,508
4	6,000	0.683	4,098
5	6,000	0.6209	3,725
6	6,000	0.5645	3,387
		NPV	6,132

PI = NPV of the project / Initial Outlay

PI = $6,132 / $20,000

PI = 0.3066

PI = 0.31

OR

$$PI = \frac{\text{PV of cash inflow}}{\text{Initial Outlay}}$$

$$PI = \frac{\$6{,}132 + \$20{,}000}{\$20{,}000}$$

$$PI = \frac{\$26{,}132}{\$20{,}000}$$

$$PI = 1.31$$

Decision rule:

Accept all projects whose PI is positive or greater than 1

May accept or reject if PI of a project = 0

10.4. Discounted Payback Period Technique (DPPT)

This technique is aimed at overcoming the problem of the time value of money by incorporating into its calculation, the discount factor. In the discounted payback period method, the cash flows are discounted and used in the calculation of payback period.

Advantages of Discounted Payback Period Technique

i. It recognizes time value of money
ii. It emphasizes on the shortness of project to payback the initial outlay.
iii. It has all the advantages of payback period aside from the fact that it recognizes time value of money.

Disadvantages of Discounted Payback Period

i. It does not take into consideration the cash inflow earned after the payback period.

ii. It does not consider risks associated with each project and the attitude of the company to risk.

ILLUSTRATION 1

A machine will cost $60,000 and will produce an annual net cash inflow of $20,000 for five years. The opportunity cost of capital is 10 percent.

Calculate the discounted payback period of the machine.

SOLUTION

Step 1

Years	Cash flows $	DF (10%)	PV $
0	-60,000	1	(60,000)
1	20,000	0.9091	18,182
2	20,000	0.8265	16,530
3	20,000	0.7513	15,026
4	20,000	0.683	13,660
5	20,000	0.6209	12,418

Step 2

Years	Cash flow	Cumulative cash flow
	$	$
0	(60,000)	(60,000)
1	18,182	(41,818)
2	16,530	(25,288)
3	15,026	(10,262)
4	13,660	
5	12,418	

Discounted Payback Period:

$= 3 \text{years} + \dfrac{10,262}{13,660} \times 12 \text{months}$

$= 3 \text{years and } 9 \text{months}$

10.5. Controversy between IRR and NPV

An "accept" or "reject" decision is one where each project may be accepted or rejected independent of what happens to other projects. NPV and IRR will always give the conclusion when applied to those projects.

In the case of mutually exclusive projects, the two methods will sometimes lead to different rankings. The conclusion here is that NPV based on discounting the return at equity cost of capital, always gives a correct ranking. The reason is that NPV indicates the immediate gain in market capitalization to equity investors.

NOTE:

NPV prevails if there is a conflict between IRR and NPV.

10.5.1. Modification of IRR

The IRR can be modified for any of the following reasons:

       b) Where the cash flows are unconventional
       c) Where projects are mutually exclusive.

However, the situation above can be taken care of by the following two methods:

   a) Extended Yield method
   b) Incremental Yield method

a)   Extended Yield Method
By this method, we modify the IRR technique in order to produce a unique IRR rather than multiple IRR. The following steps may be applied:
i. Convert the unconventional cash flow into conventional cash flows by discounting all future cash flows backwards at the given cost of capital until they are fully absorbed by the positive cash flows (cash inflows) or they become year zero cash flow.

ii. Calculate the IRR of the revised (conventional) cash flows in the normal way. This is the required IRR.

(b)   Incremental Yield Method

Where projects are mutually exclusive, it means that we cannot undertake all the projects. We must undertake only one which means that acceptance of only one project is equivalent to rejection of all other mutually exclusive projects.

IRR will produce conflicting result with NPV where mutually exclusive projects are involved because IRR does not recognize the scale or size of investments.

As a result of this, we must modify the cash flow of mutually exclusive projects, if we are mandated to evaluate them using IRR. Hence, the method for this modification is called INCREMENTAL YIELD APPROACH. Under this method, revise the cash flow to generate different or incremental cash flow. Thereafter, we calculate the IRR of these incremental cash flow and base our decision for project selection on the project that generate this incremental cash flow (i.e. the project that was kept constant)

Steps for Calculating Incremental IRR:

The following steps are to be followed in calculating the Incremental IRR.

a) Calculate the incremental cash flow by keeping one project constant (i.e. subtracting cash flow of the project from the cash flow of the project that was kept constant. e.g. project A-B if incremental cash flows are generated from A-B then A must be kept constant.

b) Calculate the IRR of these incremental cash flows in the normal way.

c) If the IRR of these incremental cash flows is greater than the company's cost of capital, then the project whose cash flow is kept constant should be accepted.

Example

Aplic Ltd's two accountants are in disagreement as to which of two mutually exclusive projects to undertake. One has based his conclusions on an IRR computation of the projects, the other based his own conclusion on NPV calculation of the projects. The required rate of return for the company is 10%.

The first project requires an investment of $705,200 and will generate net cash flows of $150,000 per annum for 10years. The second only requires $433,900 to be invested to generate $200,000 for 10years.

Required:

a) Produce the computation of the two accountants

b) Calculate IRR, by using incremental IRR

c) If the alternative investment rate was 14%, which of the two projects would be accepted?

Solution:

a) First Accountant's computation

Calculation of NPV for Project A

Years	Cash flow	D.F (10%)	PV
	$		$
0	-705,200	1	(705,200)
1 to 10	150,000	6.1446	921,690
		NPV	216,490

The present value for project A is + $216,490.

Calculation of NPV for project B

Years	Cash flow	D.F (10%)	PV
	$		$
0	-433,900	1	(433,900)
1 to 10	100,000	6.1446	614,460
		NPV	180,560

The Net Present Value of project B is +$180,560.

Decision under NPV

According to the accountant that based is decision on the outcome of computation of NPV, Project A should be accepted. The reason is that project A has +NPV of $216,490 which is greater than + NPV of $180,560.

Second accountant's computation:

Calculation of NPV for Project A

Years	Cash flow	D.F (10%)	PV
	$		$
0	-705,200	1	(705,200)
1 to 10	150,000	6.1446	921,690
		NPV	216,490

IRR for project A

Use higher rate of return to generate negative NPV.

Years	Cash flow	D.F (20%)	PV
	$		$
0	-705,200	1	(705,200)
1 to 10	150,000	4.1925	628,875
		NPV	(76,325)

IRR for project A

$$IRR = Lr + \frac{NPVLr}{NPVLr - (-NPVHr)} \times (Hr - Lr)$$

$$= 10\% + \frac{216{,}490}{216{,}490 - (-76{,}325)} \times (20 - 10)\%$$

$$= 0.1 + \frac{216{,}490}{292{,}815} \times 0.1$$

$$= 0.1 + 0.0739$$

$$= 0.1739$$

$$= 17.39\%$$

IRR for project B

Rate of return that generates + NPV.

Years	Cash flow $	D.F (10%)	PV $
0	-433,900	1	(433,900)
1 to 10	100,000	6.1446	614,460
		NPV	180,560

Use higher rate of return to generate Negative NPV

Years	Cash flow	D.F (20%)	PV
	$		$
0	-433,900	1	(433,900)
1 to 10	100,000	4.1925	419,250
		NPV	(14,650)

$$IRR = Lr + \frac{NPVLr}{NPVLr - (-NPVHr)} \times (Hr - Lr)$$

$$= 10\% + \frac{180,560}{180,560 - (-14,650)} \times (20 - 10)\%$$

$$= 10\% + \frac{180,560}{195,210} \times 10\%$$

$$= 0.1 + 0.92495 \times 0.1$$

$$= 0.1 + 0.092495$$

$$= 0.1925$$

$$= 19.25\%$$

Accountant that based his decision on the outcome of IRR will accept project B and reject project A. This is in contrary to the decision of accountant that based is decision on the outcome of NPV.

NOTE:

Whenever there is a controversy between NPV and IRR, NPV should prevail.

b) Computation of IRR, using incremental IRR

Years	A Cash flow $	B Cash flow $	Incremental cash flow(A - B) $
0	-705,200	-433,900	(271,300)
1 to 10	150,000	100,000	50,000

Rate of return that generates positive NPV:

Years	Incremental cash flow(A - B) $	D.F(10%)	PV $
0	(271,300)	1	(271,300)
1 to 10	50,000	6.1446	307,230
		NPV	35,930

Rate of return that generates Negative NPV:

Years	Incremental cash flow(A - B) $	D.F(20%)	PV $
0	(271,300)	1	(271,300)
1 to 10	50,000	4.1925	209,625

NPV   (61,675)

$$IRR = L_r + \frac{NPV_{Lr}}{NPV_{Lr} - (-NPV_{Hr})} \times (H_r - L_r)$$

$$= 10\% + \frac{35,930}{35,930 - (-61,675)} \times (20-10)\%$$

= 0.1 + 0.3681 × 0.1

= 0.1 + 0.03681

= 0.1368

= 13.68%

Decision:

Since the IRR of the incremental cash flows is greater than the company's cost of capital, it means project A, which was held constant, should be accepted. This decision is the same as the decision of the NPV.

C) If the investment rate is now 14%, it means the decision to accept project A will no more hold as the incremental IRR is less than the cost of capital of 14%. Therefore, project B, now looks more attractive and should be accepted.

CHAPTER 11

COMPLEX INVESTMENT DECISIONS

Learning Objectives

After studying this chapter, you should be able to:

      (i)   Evaluate capital projects with different lives.

      (ii)   Evaluate capital projects involving replacement and abandoning decisions

      (iii) Evaluate capital project involving inflation.

11.0. Complex Investment Decisions

Many companies are faced with complex investment decision in a practical situation. Some of the situations include choosing among investments with different lives, deciding about the replacements of an existing fixed asset and evaluating investments under inflation or capital rationing. The NPV rule can be extended to handle such situations.

11.1. Projects with Different Lives

Where mutually exclusive projects that have the same lives are being considered, the project with the highest NPV should be accepted. However, where mutually exclusive projects being considered have different lives, the use of the NPV rule without accounting for the differences in the projects' lives, may fail to indicate the correct choice. In this situation, there is need to evaluate the projects for an equal period of time to be able to arrive at a reasonable decision.

ILLUSTARATION 11.1a

A company has to choose between two grinding machines; machine Y and machine Z which are of different designs but perform the same functions. Machine Y would involve an initial cash outlay of $2,400 and operating cash expenses of $800 per year for 6 years. On the other hand, machine Z would involve an initial cash outlay of $2,000 and operating cash expenses of $1,000 per year for 3 years. If the opportunity cost of capital is 14 percent, which of the two machines should be accepted?

Hint:

The cash flows above are operating expenses, and hence they have negative figures. Initial outlay should be deducted from the present value of these operating expenses which are in negative figures. In a nutshell, it means that negative figures minus any figure, equal negative figure. For example:

- 10 - 18 = - 28

SOLUTION

Machine Y

Years	cash flow	DF (14%)	PV
	$		$
0	(2,400)	1	(2,400)
1	(800)	0.877	(702)
2	(800)	0.769	(615)
3	(800)	0.675	(540)
4	(800)	0.592	(474)
5	(800)	0.519	(415)
6	(800)	0.456	(365)
		NPV	(5,510)

Machine Z

Years	cash flow	DF (14%)	PV
	$		$
0	(2,000)	1	(2,000)
1	(1,000)	0.877	(877)
2	(1,000)	0.769	(769)
3	(1,000)	0.675	(675)
		NPV	(4,321)

If the difference in the project lives is disregarded, machine Z will be chosen since it has lower present value of costs. This is not a good decision for a company taking into consideration that machine Y will last for 6 years and machine Z will last for 3 years and will need to be replaced at the end of the third year.

ILLUSTRATION 11.1b

Using illustration 11.1a and assuming that machine M is replaced at the end of the 3rd year at the same initial outlay and same operating expenses and life expectancy, the new position would be as follows:

Machine Y

Years	cash flow	DF (14%)	PV
	$		$
0	(2,400)	1	(2,400)
1	(800)	0.877	(702)
2	(800)	0.769	(615)

	3	(800)		0.675	(540)
	4	(800)		0.592	(474)
	5	(800)		0.519	(415)
	6	(800)		0.456	(365)
			NPV		(5,510)

Machine Z

Years	cash flow $	DF (14%)	PV $
0	(2,000)	1	(2,000)
1	(1,000)	0.877	(877)
2	(1,000)	0.769	(769)
3	(3,000)	0.675	(2,025)
4	(1,000)	0.592	(592)
5	(1,000)	0.519	(519)
6	(1,000)	0.456	(456)
			(7,238)

By the end of year 6, machine Y will need to be replaced for the first time while machine Z would need to be replaced the second time. When the NPVs of the two machines are compared at the end of year 6, machine Y would be chosen. It is clearly shown here that the use of simple NPV rule will produce wrong decision when two projects with different lives are considered.

It is advisable to put into consideration the project lives when taking the decision. The best method of evaluating these types of projects is called Annual Equivalent Value.

Annual Equivalent Value (AEV) is the NPV of an investment divided by annuity factor given its rate and discounts.

$$AEV = \frac{NPV}{\text{Annuity Factor}}$$

Note:

Annuity factor is the sum of the discounting factor starting from year 1 up to the discounting factor of the last year of the project.

This method can be best used where there is absent of inflation as it is quicker and less cumbersome than any other method.

ILLUSTRATION 11.1c

Using illustration 11.1a, the result will be as follows:

Machine Y

Years	cash flow	DF (14%)	PV
	$		$
0	(2,400)	1	(2,400)
1	(800)	0.877	(702)
2	(800)	0.769	(615)
3	(800)	0.675	(540)
4	(800)	0.592	(474)
5	(800)	0.519	(415)
6	(800)	0.456	(365)
		3.888	(5,510)

Machine Z

Years	cash flow	DF (14%)	PV

	$		$
0	(2,000)	1	(2,000)
1	(1,000)	0.877	(877)
2	(1,000)	0.769	(769)
3	(1,000)	0.675	(675)
		2.321	(4,321)

Calculation of Annual Equivalent Value for Machine Y and Z are as follows:

AEV for machine Y = $\dfrac{\$5{,}510}{3.888}$

$\qquad\qquad\qquad = \$1{,}417.18$

AEV for machine Z = $\dfrac{\$4{,}321}{2.321}$

$\qquad\qquad\qquad = \$1{,}861.7$

Decision:
Machine Y should be chosen because it has lower AEV of cost ($1,417.18) when compared with AEV of cost ($1,861.7) of Machine Z. This is in agreement with illustration 11.1b

11. 2   Replacement and Abandonment Decisions

The method of constant replacement chains to choose between assets with different lives was discussed in the previous section. It was discussed that assets are replaced at the end of their economic lives but this is not always the case in practice.

Replacement of asset should be intelligently planned. You need to consider the economic benefits (cash inflow) of the old asset you intend to replace or abandon with a new machine you plan to accept.

Some organizations follow the practice of approving a new machine only when the existing one can no longer work properly. This is one of the most expensive policies which a business entity could follow. A professional analysis may indicate replacement of a machine when it is, say 6 years old with an improved new machine. However, if the machine is retained till when it is beyond repairs, say 17 years, the company must have been incurring extra expenditures on maintenance and losing extra profit for 11years. A company that follow this practice is likely to fold up if care is not taken as it will be unable to compete favourably with companies that adopt cost-reduction policies by adopting a systematic replacement policy and rule.

In conclusion, for a company to remain in business it should adopt a replacement policy based on economic consideration and decide when to replace.

ILLUSTARTION 11.2

Supposing a company is operating a machine which is expected to produce net cash inflows of $2,500,000, $2,000,000, $1,500,000, $1,000,000 for the next 4 years. A new machine which is more efficient to operate and cost effective has just been introduced into the market. It is expected that the new machine will cost $7,500,000 and will generate a net cash inflow of $3,500,000 a year for six years. What should the company do?

SOLUTION

Old Machine

Years	cash flow	DF (14%)	PV	AEV
	$'000		$'000	$'000
0		1		

1	2,500	0.877	2,193	1,831.45	
2	2,000	0.769	1,538	1,831.45	
3	1,500	0.675	1,013	1,831.45	
4	1,000	0.592	592	1,831.45	
		2.913	5,335		

New Machine

Years	cash flow $'000	DF (14%)	PV $'000	AEV $'000
0	7,500	1	(7,500)	1,570.99
1	3,500	0.877	3,070	1,570.99
2	3,500	0.769	2,692	1,570.99
3	3,500	0.675	2,363	1,570.99
4	3,500	0.592	2,072	1,570.99
5	3,500	0.519	1,817	1,570.99
6	3,500	0.456	1,596	1,570.99
		3.888	6,108	

The table above shows that a chain of the cash flow for the new machine is equivalent to an annuity of ($6,108,000 ÷ 3.888) = $ 1,570,990 per year for the life of the machine. The old machine generates an annuity of ($5,335,000 ÷ 2.913) = $1,831,450.

Decision:

The old machine should not be replaced by the new machine because the annual equivalent value in cash inflow of the old machine ($1,831,450) is higher than that of the new machine ($1,570,990).

11.3 Inflation in Capital Budgeting

Inflation is a vital factor of the economic and must be considered in capital budgeting. It is an increase in estimate as a result of changes in price level. The impact of inflation should be correctly included in the investment in order to prevent errors. If we ignore inflation, we may end up overstating or understating our net cash flows in which case the NPVs used for decision making would be wrong.

11.3.1 Relevant Concepts

Inflation can be incorporated in capital budgeting by the usage of any of the following two concepts:

(a) Nominal rate or Money cost of capital
(b) Real rate or real cost of capital

Concept of Nominal rate or Money Cost of capital

The nominal rate is the normal cost of capital of a company which would have been calculated subject to money market rate of interest of the providers of capital or funds. It is the cost of capital that has not been adjusted for inflation. Where cash flows are inflated, or incorporates inflation, or are given in money terms, we should discount such cash flows using the money cost of capital.

Concept of Real Rate or Real Cost of Capital

The real rate of capital is the cost of capital that has been adjusted for inflation.

The impact of inflation in investment appraisal (capital budgeting) could be adjusted for, either in the discounting rate (cost of capital) or cash flow. The discount rate is usually determined by the market and stated in nominal terms.

However, where discount rates are expressed in real terms, they can be reversed to their nominal value through the following which is known as Fisher's effect in economic theory.

Nominal rate = (1+ Real Rate) (1+ Inflation Rate) – 1

This equation can also be used to derive the real rate of return thus:

Real Rate = $\frac{(1+\text{Nominal Rate})}{(1+\text{Inflation Rate})} - 1$

If discount rate is stated in nominal terms, then cash flow must also be estimated in nominal terms. This is called consistency.

Some costs are more sensitive to inflation than others. Certain items are not affected by inflation, for instance the tax shield on depreciation (for tax purpose depreciation is not allowed on the book value). In evaluating viability of a project, the real cash flow could be discounted at real discount rate, or the nominal cash flows discounted at the nominal rate.

Both methods will always give the same answers subject to approximation error.

ILLUSTRATION

AY Ltd. forecasts the following project cash flows in real terms and discount at a 15% nominal rate. Should the firm invest in it if 10% rate of inflation is assumed?

	Year 0	Year 1	Year 2	Year 3
	$	$	$	$
cash flow	20,000	7,000	10,000	6,000

SUGESTED SOLUTION

Alternative I: Converting real cash flows to nominal terms

Years	Real Cash Flow	Workings	Nominal Cash Flows

	$	$	$
0	20,000	20,000(1)	=20,000
1	7,000	7,000(1+ 0.1)¹	=7,700
2	10,000	10,000(1+0.1)²	=12,100
3	6,000	6,000(1+0.1)³	=7,986

Computation of NPV

Years	Nominal Cash Flow $	D.F (15%)	PV $
0	-20,000	1	-20,000
1	7,700	0.8696	6,696
2	12,100	0.7561	9,149
3	7,986	0.6575	5,251
		NPV	1,096

Note: The discount rate is already in nominal term. You do not need to convert it to nominal term.

Alternative II: Converting nominal rate to real rate

Real rate = $\dfrac{1 + \text{Nominal rate}}{1 + \text{Inflation rate}} - 1$

$= \dfrac{1 + 0.15}{1 + 0.1} - 1$

$= 4.55\%$

Year	Cash flow $	D.F (4.55%)	PV $
0	(20,000)	1	(20,000)
1		0.9565	

	7,000		6,696
2	10,000	0.9149	9,149
3	6,000	0.875	5,250
		NPV	1,095

The NPV of the project is $1,095

Decision rule: The project should be accepted because the NPV of the project is positive $1,095. It can be seen that NPV in the two alternative computations are almost equal.

CHAPTER 12

CAPITAL RATIONING

Learning Objectives

After studying this chapter, you should be able to:

(i) Evaluate capital projects under single period capital rationing.

(ii) Know the meaning of multi-period capital rationing and setting up of linear programming equation.

Capital Rationing

Capital rationing arises when there are insufficient funds to execute all available and profitable projects. The inadequacy of resources to finance projects may arise due to external factors or internal constraints imposed by management.

Capital rationing situation is on in which a company does not have sufficient funds to execute worthwhile investment projects. Under this situation, a company has projects with positive NPV whose combined outlays exceed all available finance to the company for the same period.

Capital rationing is the technique for selecting projects during a period of funds restriction which normally requires the ranking of projects in a descending order of desirability and accepting them in that order until all available funds have been exhausted.

12.1 Single Period Capital Rationing

This is where restriction is for only one period. We must use profitability index to select projects where restriction is for only one year.

12.2 Profitability Index (PI)

This concept is based on the contribution per limiting factor approach. It is actually a benefit/cost analysis of projects. It can be measured by the ratio of Gross Present Value (GPV) of a project to the outlay required for the project during the year of restriction.

The formulas for calculating profitability index are mentioned below:

Profitability Index (PI)

$$= \frac{\text{Gross Present Value}}{\text{Initial Outlay}}$$

Or

$$= \frac{\text{NPV} + \text{Initial Outlay}}{\text{Initial Outlay}}$$

Steps to be taken in single period capital rationing situation are as follows:

1. Identify the year of restriction.
2. Calculate the PV and NPV of the projects (if not given)
3. Rank all projects using P.I.
4. Allocate available funds to projects in a descending order of P.I
5. If a project does not require outlay during the year of restriction, its P.I would be an infinite sum (NPV + 0) and such projects must be ranked first and must be selected first.

ILLUSTRATION 1

Suppose a company is faced with a problem of investing $500,000 in three projects which are all attractive and profitable @12 percent opportunity cost of capital. Which of the projects should be undertaken, given the following evaluation results?

Projects	Initial Outlay $	NPV @ 12% $

1	500,000	105,000
2	250,000	80,000
3	250,000	60,000

SUGGESTED SOLUTION

Calculation of profitability Index (P.I)

P.I = $\frac{\text{NPV + Initial Outlay}}{\text{Initial Outlay}}$

= PV/Initial Outlay
Profitability Index (P.I)

Project 1 = $\frac{\$105,000 + \$500,000}{\$500,000}$

= 1.21

Project 2 = $\frac{\$80,000 + \$250,000}{\$250,000}$

= 1.32

Project 3 = $\frac{\$60,000 + \$250,000}{\$250,000}$

= 1.24

Projects	Initial Outlay $	NPV @ 12% $	P.I	Ranking using NPV	Ranking using P.I
1	500,000	105,000	1.21	1	3
2	250,000	80,000	1.32	2	1
3	250,000	60,000	1.24	3	2

The above table shows that the three projects are viable and should be undertaken if there is no capital constraint, but the question states that the company has only $500,000 to invest.

Using the NPV rule, the firm will accept project 1 which has NPV of $105,000, and initial outlay of $500,000 that exhausts the available fund, but the use of P.I suggests otherwise. The P.I suggests the selection of project 2 and 3 which together have higher NPV of $140,000 ($80,000+ $60,000) and total initial outlay of $500,000 ($250,000 + $250,000).

Allocation of funds according to the profitability index:

	$
Available funds	500,000
Select project 1	(250,000)
	250,000
Select project 2	(250,000)
	Nil

In conclusion, where there is insufficient fund or resources to execute all the viable project, profitability index should be used in ranking the project and not NPV.

ILLUSTRATION 2

Miami Ltd. has a capital budget of $250,000 for the year to June 30, 2003. The available projects have been identified and quantified by the technical director and the works manager as listed below. The individual project's related profitability index has been computed by a financial management team and stated below:

Projects	Initial Outlay $	P.I
A	125,000	1.1

B	50,000	0.95
C	100,000	1.25
D	100,000	1.23
E	125,000	1.05
F	50,000	1.2
G	25,000	0.99

(a) Which projects should the company invest in?

(b) What difference would the absence of capital rationing make to your selection in "a" above?

SUGGESTED SOLUTION

(a)

Projects	Initial Outlay $	P.I	Ranking
A	125,000	1.1	4th
B	50,000	0.95	7th
C	100,000	1.25	1st
D	100,000	1.23	2nd
E	125,000	1.05	5th
F	50,000	1.2	3rd
G	25,000	0.99	6th

Allocation of funds:

	$
Available funds	250,000
Allocation to project C	(100,000)
	150,000
Allocation to project D	(100,000)
	50,000
Allocation to project F	(50,000)
	-

Miami Ltd. should invest in projects C, D and F in that order of priority.

(b)

Calculation of Present Value (GPV or PV)

P.I = PV/I.O

PV= P.I x I.O
Where:
P.I = profitability Index
PV = Present Value
I.O = Initial Outlay

Projects	P.I	I.O $	PV= P.I X I.O $	NPV= PV -I.O $
A	1.1	125,000	137,500	12,500
B	0.95	50,000	47,500	(2,500)
C	1.25	100,000	125,000	25,000
D	1.23	100,000	123,000	23,000
E	1.05	125,000	131,250	6,250
F	1.2	50,000	60,000	10,000
G	0.99			

25,000	24,750	(250)

Decision rule:

If there is no capital rationing, the company should undertake all projects with positive NPV. In this case, the company should invest in all projects except projects B and G which have negative NPV.

12.3 Different Situation of Capital Rationing

The different situations of capital rationing are as follows:
(a) Where projects are divisible
(b) Where projects are indivisible
(c) Where projects are mutually dependent
(d) Where projects are mutually exclusive

Divisible Projects

In this case, there is an implicit linearity assumption between the initial outlays and the NPV's of a product. This follows from the basic assumption that fraction of a project can be undertaken. Therefore, a fractional investment in the outlay would yield a proportionate fractional return in NPV. For example, investment of 20% in the outlay, would yield 20% of NPV.

Indivisible Projects

The assumption in this case is that projects are not divisible fractions and cannot therefore be undertaken in parts. It is only in this case that there may be surplus of funds which represents the available funds after allocation.

ILLUSTARTION 3

Amazeno Ltd. is experiencing a shortage of funds for investment in the current year, when only $50,000 is available for investment. No fund shortages are foreseen thereafter. The cost of investing fund is 20%. The following projects are available:

Projects	1	2	3	4	5	6
Initial Outlay	$25,000	$40,000	$30,000	$15,000	$12,500	$20,000
Annual receipts to Perpetuity	$7,500	$10,000	$9,000	$5,000	$4,000	$5,000

You are required to advise management on the projects which you would recommend for acceptance if they were:

(a) Divisible
(b) Indivisible

SUGGESTED SOLUTION

Projects	Initial Outlay	PV	P.I	Ranking
1	$25,000	$37,500	1.5	3rd
2	$40,000	$50,000	1.25	6th
3	$30,000	$45,000	1.5	4th
4	$15,000	$25,000	1.67	1st
5	$12,500	$20,000	1.6	2nd
6	$20,000	$25,000	1.25	5th

(a) Allocation of available funds where projects are divisible:

	$
Available fund	50,000
Allocation to project 4	(15,000)
	35,000
Allocation to project 5	(12,500)
	22,500

| Allocate (56.25%) to project 1 | (22,500) |
| | Nil |

(b) Allocation of available funds where projects are indivisible:

	$
Available fund	50,000
Allocation to project 4	(15,000)
	35,000
Allocation to project 5	(12,500)
	22,500
Allocation to project 6	(20,000)
Surplus funds	2,500

Since projects are indivisible, management should accept projects 4, 5 and 6.

Project 1 which is the 3rd on the ranking should be replaced by project 6 which is the next on the ranking because project 1 is higher ($25,000) than the available balance of fund ($22,500) and according to the question, funds should not be allocated to the fractional part of a project.

Workings:

Calculation of present value for each project:

$PV = A \times 1/r$

Project 1   = $7,500 x 1/0.2
            = $37,500

Project 2   = $10,000 x 1/0.2
            = $50.000

Project 3   = $9,000 x 1/0.2
            = $45,000

Project 4   = $5,000 x 1/0.2
            = $25,000

Project 5   = $4,000 x 1/0.2
            = $20.000

Project 6   = $5,000 x 1/0.2
            = $25,000

Calculation of profitability Index for each project:

P.I = PV/I.O

P.I for project 1 = $37,500/$25,000
                  = 1.5

P.I for project 2 = $50,000/$40,000
                  = 1.25

P.I for project 3 = $45,000/30,000
                  = 1.5

P.I for project 4 = $25,000/$15,000
                  = 1.67

P.I for project 5 = $20,000/$12,500
                  = 1.6

P.I for project 6 = $25,000/$20,000
                  = 1.25

Where:

PV = Present Value
A = Annual receipt from project
r = Cost of investing funds
I.O = Initial Outlay

Mutually Dependent Projects

In this case, acceptance of one of the mutually dependent projects automatically implies an acceptance of the remaining mutually dependent project. For example, if projects A and B are mutually dependent, it means that the two projects can either be accepted jointly or rejected together.

Mutually Exclusive Projects

In this case, an acceptance of one project group implies the rejection of all other project group. This issue can be resolved by modifying the ranking procedures and it is done as follows:

(iv) create as many groups of projects as long as they are mutually exclusive. This can be done by ensuring that each group contains only one of the mutually exclusive projects and would of course exclude the others.

(v) rank and select projects in each group

(vi) calculate the total NPVs of the selected projects in each group.

(vii) the decision would be to accept projects from the groups that produce maximum total NPVs.

ILLUSTRATION 4

Jeff and Smith have just received their gratuities which amounted to $2,000,000 and they are prepared to invest in a new venture PZI Ltd. A bank has expressed the desire to grant them long-term loan of up to $10,000,000. They have presented the following investment proposals to you for financial advice.

Projects	A	B	C	D	E	F	G	H	I	J
P.I	1.17	1.2	1.19	1.22	1.15	1.15	1.22	1.20	1.16	1.10
Outlay($'million)	2.00	3.00	1.50	4.00	4.00	2.00	1.00	1.50	1.00	3.00

The company expected cost of capital is 15%. Project B and C are mutually exclusive while projects A and D are mutually dependent.

(a) As a financial adviser, what projects would you recommend? Assume that fractions of a project can be undertaken.

SUGGESTED SOLUTION
Group A (includes project B but excluding project C)
Ranking

Projects	P.I	I.O	P.I X I.O PV	PV - I.O NPV
		$'000	$'000	$'000
G	1.22	1,000	1,220	220
H	1.2	1500	1,800	300
B	1.2	3000	3,600	600
A&D	1.2	6000	7,200	1,200
I	1.16	1000	1,160	160
F	1.15	2000	2,300	300
E	1.15	4000	4,600	600
J	1.1	3000	3,300	300

Allocation of funds to the projects according to P.I ranking:

NPV

	$'000	$,000
Available funds	12,000	
Select project G	(1,000)	220
	11,000	
Select project H	(1,500)	300
	9,500	
Select project B	(3,000)	600
	6,500	
Select project A & D	(6,000)	1,200
	500	
Select 50% of project I	(500)	80
	Nil	2,400

The total NPV = $2,400,000
This group includes B but exclude C because the two projects are mutually exclusive while project "A" and "D" are mutually dependent.

Group B (Including project C but excluding project B)

Ranking Projects	P.I	1.O $'000	P.I X 1.O PV $'000	PV - 1.O NPV $'000
G	1.22	1,000	1,220	220
H	1.2	1,500	1,800	300
A&D	1.2	6,000	7,200	1,200
C	1.19	1,500	1785	285
I	1.16	1,000	1,160	160

F	1.15	2,000	2,300	300	
E	1.15	4,000	4,600	600	
J	1.1	3,000	3,300	300	

Allocation of funds to the projects according to P.I ranking:

	$'000	NPV $,000
Available funds	12,000	
Select project G	(1,000)	220
	11,000	
Select project H	(1,500)	300
	9,500	
Select project A & D	(6,000)	1,200
	3,500	
Select project C	(1,500)	285
	2,000	
Select project I	(1,000)	160
	1,000	
Select 50% of project F	(1,000)	150
	Nil	2,315

The total NPV = $2,315,000

This group includes C but exclude B because the two projects are mutually exclusive while project "A" and "D" are mutually dependent.

Decision

The company is advised to choose projects G, H, B, A&D and 50% of project I (Group A) because they produced the higher NPV of $2,400,000 compared to that of group "B" of $2,315,000.

NOTE: The profitability Index for A&D is calculated as follows:

$$P.I = \frac{(1.17 \times \$2\text{million}) + (1.22 \times \$4\text{million})}{\$2\text{million} + \$4\text{million}}$$

$$= \frac{\$2.34 + \$4.88\text{million}}{\$6\text{million}}$$

$$= 1.20$$

12.4 Multi-Period Capital Rationing or Funds Constraints Problems

Where capital is restricted in more than one period, a formulation of linear programming is required to select projects which will maximise the NPVs for the company.
Capital investment decision under multi-period funds constraint situations have the objectives of choosing a combination of projects which gives the firm maximum total net present value, subject to company's resources availability.

ILLUSRATION 1

PYZ consult has identified the following projects:

Projects	year 0 $	Year 1 $	Year 2 $
A	(100,000)	(100,000)	302,410
B	(50,000)	(100,000)	218,070
C	(200,000)	150,000	107,230

Provide a mathematical programming formulation to assist the company in choosing the most viable project if capital available for year 0 and year1 is limited to $170,000 and $80,000 respectively. Assume 5 percent cost of capital and that the projects are divisible.

SUGGESTED SOLUTION

Project A

years	Cash Flow $	DF 5%	PV $
0	(100,000)	1	(100,000)
1	(100,000)	0.952	(95,200)
2	302,410	0.907	274,286
		NPV	79,086

Project B

years	Cash Flow $	DF 5%	PV $
0	(50,000)	1	(50,000)
1	(100,000)	0.952	(95,200)
2	218,070	0.907	197,789
		NPV	52,589

Project C

years	Cash	DF	PV

	Flow $	5%	$
0	(200,000)	1	(200,000)
1	150,000	0.952	142,800
2	107,230	0.907	97,258
		NPV	40,058

Maximize NPV = $79,086A + 52,589B + 40,058C

Subject to:

$100,000A + $50,000B + $200,000C ≤ $170,000

$100,000A + $100,000B ≤ $80,000 + $150,000C

$$A, B, C \leq 1$$
$$A, B, C \geq 0$$

NOTE: The above equation can be solved using the computer.

12.5 Limitation of Linear/integer programming

(a) very technical

(b) can only be solved with the help of computer

(c) very costly to use when large indivisible projects are involved

(d) it assumes that future investment opportunities are known.

12.6 Limitation of Capital Rationing

The following are the limitation of capital rationing

(a) The assumption of divisibility of projects may not be possible in practice, for all projects

(b) The assumptions of linearity in initial outlay and NPV of projects may not hold because of the economies and diseconomies of scale.

(c) On many occasions capital rationing treats projects in isolation in more. It does not recognise the interdependence of projects.

12.7 Summary and Conclusion

Capital rationing situation is a situation in which a company does not have enough funds or resources to finance all available viable projects. Many methods have been devised to solve both single period capital rationing and multi-period capital rationing.

References:

ICAN (2009) Strategic Financial Management

Toye Adelaja (2016) Capital budgeting

www.accountinghour.com

www.ingramcontent.com/pod-product-compliance
Lightning Source LLC
Chambersburg PA
CBHW071819200526
45169CB00018B/445